ROCKY ROAD
TO DEMOCRACY

A struggle with legacy of two totalitarian regimes

Author: Veronika Valdova

Motto:

No nation ever became great by killing off its best people

DEDICATION

This book is dedicated to Major Jan Beneš (26th March 1936 – 1st June 2007), for his distinguished service for the U.S. Department of Defense after his emigration from Communist Czechoslovakia, and the inspiration he provided to those he understood the cost of life in liberty.

CONTENTS

ACKNOWLEDGMENTS

I started working on this manuscript in May 2011, when I returned to the Czech Republic after a rather adventurous period in the United Kingdom. Due to certain peculiarities of UK law which allowed local authorities to treat a whistleblower in industrial safety as a highly dangerous undesirable element, I had to use all my previously undeclared life experience to survive and get out of that mess alive. This book would never be written if it was not for self-less help of people whose names I do not know, but who were immensely helpful by providing assistance and guidance during all those joint anti-terrorist exercises I inadvertently became part of; and later, during the creative process, by making comments, sending references to truly unique websites, reviewing the text as I wrote it, suggesting alternative explanations, and providing the most interesting documents they could find. In this sense, this little book is a true result of common effort. Special thanks belongs to Mike the Ranger for his fairy-tale story about Rangers who were run over by whole village of really ruthless Cannibal natives in an incredibly ugly jungle, and their survival strategy; and to SF Weapons Sergeant Dallas.

Veronika Valdova

ABSTRACT

This paper is an unofficial overview of constitutional development of Czechoslovakia, key historical events, and points which I personally consider critical in its democratic development. This book does not represent point of view of any official authority. It is my personal attempt to get straight the events and their meaning, to the best of my current understanding and ability.

Transition of Eastern European countries from Communism to democracy has not been painless and without affairs. Twenty years from abolition of one Party rule, it is time for a serious reflection of what has been accomplished, and where are the most serious areas of concern. Communist Czechoslovakia, after the Velvet Revolution (1989) and the breaking off Slovakia (1992), was transformed into a country with multiparty democracy with proportional representation in two-chamber Parliament; became a member of NATO (1999) and the European Union (2004); and its economy compared to other European countries is doing reasonably well. As most other small players, the Czech Republic seldom appears on international political scene with anything of significance.

This paper discusses history of Czechoslovakia in international context, and presents some not widely known international agreements signed by the exile government of Edvard Beneš. Czechoslovakia during its short history became part of two authoritarian empires, first as Protectorate of Nazi Germany and second as a Soviet satellite; and its road to democracy was littered by hundreds of thousands of bodies of civilians slaughtered at time of peace. This text was inspired by Robert A Dahl's paper "What institutions does large scale democracy require?" which was published in PSQ, Vol. 120, No 2; summer 2005.

The first section briefly presents constitutional development of Czechoslovakia from the end of WW1 until 1992, and explains the most important changes introduced by the respective governments. Analytical part of this section takes the conditions of poly-archal democracy as explained in Dahl's paper and applies his conclusions to the situation in Czechoslovakia. The purpose of this paper is to try to identify the main reasons why the "project Czechoslovakia" went so terribly wrong.

Second section presents observations of critical incidents in the history of Czechoslovakia. This overview is very brief and emphasizes only incidents which I personally consider key turning points.

Sections three and four are dedicated to identification of possible design flaws in the electoral system itself, namely when it comes to its substantive meaning; and to the power of media in a closed society seriously constrained by language barrier.

The fifth, concluding part, compares my observations to the Dahl's principles of poly-archal democracy, and defines conditions which can potentially prove critical for further democratic development. The system can have many formal characteristics of democracy, and be in fact a ruthless authoritarian regime with high level of democide. The paper is meant to contribute to the discussion what is the difference between democratic and authoritarian regimes, and to help identify conditions which directly lead to tyranny.

The Appendix contains two long forgotten bilateral agreements between Czechoslovakia and USSR from World War Two, substantive excerpt from the Košice Government Program, and analysis "Background to Czechoslovak crisis" by former U.S. Ambassador to Czechoslovakia Laurence A Steinhardt.

1 CONSTITUTION & DEMOCRACY

The first document to check when one comes to study of political regimes is Constitution of the concerned state, as it defines origins of power in the state, its division and control, and also rights and responsibilities of its subjects. There are several very interesting points in constitutional development of Czechoslovakia. The fact that there was a historical period later defined as "non-freedom" (from September 1938 to May 1945[I]), which brought in power two independently functioning governments: Hácha's Protectorate[1] puppet government and Beneš's government in exile[2], respectively, resulted in constitutional improvisation[3] after the war[II].

From constitutional development perspective, the most stunning is the fact that some agreements and Constitutional Acts were **retrospectively declared invalid**; namely the Munich Agreement, the Wien Award, abdication[4, 5] of Edvard Beneš, and all constitutional and other acts of the Hácha's Protectorate government during the period from September 30, 1940 to May 4, 1945[III]. Moreover, some Presidential Decrees issued by the exile government of Edvard Beneš became Constitutional Acts: 15 Constitutional Decrees from the period 21 July 1940 to 27 October 1945 through Act 57/1946[6]. This, together with the very formation of the exile government and its recognition, resulted in awkward legal status of the exile and first post-war cabinet. William Curtiss examined in detail **dubious legitimacy of the exile government**, and compared the situation to the principles of Max Weber[IV].

[I] Košice Government Program was signed in April 1945.

[II] Great Britain recognized Edvard Beneš's exile government on July 18, 1941; USSR a month later on August 17, 1941. Emil Hácha was elected by the Syrový's Cabinet in November 1938, when Czechoslovakia still functioned as an independent nation. Protectorate was established only in March 1939.

[III] Abdication of Edvard Beneš was declared invalid, Beneš returns in office. Edvard Beneš accepted the office of president, despite his abdication of 5 October 1938. It was said to have been forced through violence, and therefore invalid. Beneš's mandate, which was to have expired under the constitution of the first republic in 1942, was extended by a decision of the government, until the time the National Assembly could meet and re-elect the head of state. (The paths of Czech constitutionality, 2010).

[IV] Czechoslovakia gained its independence out of Austro-Hungarian Empire without a fight. National renewal movement was only cultural, and the only armed conflict the

3

The **Munich Agreement**[7] was declared as void by Great Britain, France, and Italy on August 5, 1942; General De Gaulle's government in exile declared it null ab initio in September 1942, and the new Italian government dissociated itself from the Munich Agreement in September 1944. Nuremberg Tribunal[8] 1946 declared it null and void as of September 30, 1946; and finally in 1973 the Treaty of Prague between Czechoslovakia and the Federal Republic of Germany declared the Munich Agreement to be null and void[9]. The Signatories also agreed that their borders were inviolable and that they would not use force against one another. The context and legal reasoning behind this decision of the Nuremberg War Crimes Tribunal is explained in detail in The Nuremberg Trial and International Law by George A Finch[10].

Another point is the fact that Czechoslovak **Constitution is a poly-legal one**, what means that there are numerous Acts and other norms which are in fact part of the Constitution. The most important problem of too lengthy and complex Constitution is that it makes taking an **oath** while entering public service of any kind obsolete. This can be compared to the situation in Great Britain, where Constitution as a single document does not exist; and the system relies on statutes such as Magna Carta 1215 and the Act of Settlement 1701, laws and customs of Parliament, political conventions, case law, coronation oath, and loyalty to the monarch[11, 12]. The Constitution 1960 replaced the previous text of the oath from "loyalty to the Constitution and its laws, and its people's democratic regime, to the benefit of the people and the state" as defined in the 1948 Constitution[V] to primary loyalty to the "Czechoslovak socialist republic

---

Czechoslovaks got involved in was tiny minority of deserters who formed the Czechoslovak legion. The perceived illegitimacy was then fully utilized by the angry German minority for subversion of the state, and later occupation of the nation, again, without firing a shot. After his resignation, Beneš was considered by Americans a "controversial figure removed from his powerbase with few friends". Beneš's popularity increased with every aggressive step of the Hitler government and had little to do with his cabinet's actions. Americans provided limited recognition to the "Czech National Committee"; however, many distinguished diplomats including George Kennan advised against it and opted for support of domestic resistance around Hácha. (W Curtiss: Manufacturing legitimacy. The Czechoslovak exile government 1938-48).

V Oath from the Constitution 1948: " I pledge my allegiance to the Republic of Czechoslovakia and its people's democratic regime. I will preserve its laws and will conduct my mandate in line with my conscience for the benefit of the people and the state."

and the cause of socialism"[VI]. The original statement from the Constitution 1920 required loyalty to the "Czechoslovak Republic, its laws, and ones conscience"[VII].

Enlightened understanding of the foundations of the system by majority of population is one of key conditions of functional democracy, because, especially in hierarchical organizations, it allows a public servant, or a member of the military, to refuse to follow an order which is not lawful, with reasonable confidence that he or she won't be removed for disobedience.

In environment, where most people do not understand fundamental standards, or where these are not effectively enforceable in real time, people cannot challenge the authority which delegates an unlawful order to lower ranks. This situation creates conditions for exploitation of hierarchical systems by providing no real guidance or standards of government, management, or command. During the **Nuremberg trials**[13] with Nazi War criminals, the defense was mostly based on the lack of understanding of "rules of civility and ethical conduct in science",[14, 15] and the requirement to follow orders. Constitution has to be part of educational standard, to become a document which everyone knows and most people understand, and not a topic for a few specialized lawyers and academics.

1.1   Brief overview of constitutional development in Czechoslovakia

This is not a paper on constitutional development; however, I wish to make a few points I consider crucial on the journey from relatively solid foundations through two totalitarian regimes back to well defined democratic constitution. There is something peculiar in the mindset of leaders who for whatever reason decide to choose a route of killing and

---

VI Oath from the Constitution 1960: "I promise on my honor and conscience that I will remain faithful to the Czechoslovak Socialist Republic and the cause of socialism. I will follow the will of the people and the interests of the people, and the Constitution and other acts of the Republic, and work toward its materialization in real life." This is the version written by Rychetský and Jičínský. Oath from the 1960 constitution was undertaken by Václav Havel at his first presidency.

VII Oath from the Constitution 1920: "I pledge my allegiance to the Republic of Czechoslovakia, and promise to preserve legality, and to conduct my mandate in line with my best knowledge and conscience".

expulsion of large groups of population, and even define such intention in basic documents of the state.

1.1.1   American origins of the Constitution of Czechoslovakia

In the beginning of the Great War, in October 1915, delegates of the Slovak League and the Czech National Association signed a proclamation declaring determination of Czechs and Slovaks to fight for their own national state against the Austrian-Hungarian Empire. As the document was signed in Cleveland, Ohio, it later became known as the **Cleveland Agreement**[16]. In May 1918, after the War, it was replaced by the **Pittsburgh Agreement**[17], which defined the newly established state as a republic with democratic Constitution. In the **Washington Declaration**[18] Czechoslovak representation accepted the ideals of modern democracy based on American principles as defined in the Declaration of Independence and the Bill of Rights. The document was drafted in Washington on October 16, 1918, and signed in Paris by Tomas Garrigue Masaryk, Milan Rastislav Štefánik, and Edvard Beneš two days later.

The newly established state was defined as secular democratic republic with universal suffrage, freedom of expression, religion, science, and associational autonomy; and equal rights of women and minorities[19]. Regular military was supposed to be replaced by militia, and hereditary titles and privileges would be cancelled to allow series of economic and social reforms. Several days later, on October 26, 1918, the **Philadelphian Agreement**[20] defined acquisition of Ruthenia. On October 30, 1918, the so-called **Martin Declaration**[21] redefined some aspects of the status of Slovakia within the new state[22], but later became subject to disputes as many participants did not consider the document valid because of unauthorized amendments made in the last minute by Milan Hodza. From the origin of the foundation documents, the God-Fathers of Czechoslovak democracy[23] can easily be traced to the USA.

1.1.2   Swiss intermezzo

On November 13, 1918, the National Assembly adopted Act 37/1918 as the **Interim Constitution**[24] of the Republic of Czechoslovakia. The newly established Revolutionary National Assembly was based on the National Committee by cooptation of 256 members of Parliament by political parties using results of elections to the Austrian-Hungarian Empire Council from 1911. President, as well as the government, was elected by the National Assembly. The first, Interim, Constitution established unity of executive and legislative power following the example of Switzerland[25]. The state form was not defined in the Interim Constitution, although it did define that e.g. the court verdicts would be issued in the name of Republic. Unity of executive and legislative power which came from the Swiss document without the part relating to direct democracy (as suggested by Petr Cibulka after 1989) is exactly the point which later became a serious problem during the first post-war cabinet of Edvard Beneš.

1.1.3   Back to the Godfathers

The **Constitution from 1920**[26] written by a team led by Prof Jiri Hoetzel was based on the Constitution of the USA[27], December Constitution of the Austrian-Hungarian Empire (1867)[28], and Constitution of the Third French Republic[29]. This Constitution created a parliamentary republic with legislative, executive, and judicial power strictly divided. The executive branch was formed by the government and the office of president, and the legislative branch was meant to exercise power through two-chamber National Assembly, which consisted of 300 members of Parliament who were elected in office for 6 years, and 150 Senators who were elected for 8 years. The president was elected for 7 years, and there was an exception in limitation to two terms for Tomas Garrigue Masaryk. The suffrage was universal, with active right to vote from 26 years, and passive right from 45 except for the office of president where the minimum age limit was 35 years.

The **"Interim state regime"** was formed by the exile government and President Edvard Beneš (from 9 July 1940[VIII] to 27 October 1945), and the **State Council** (from 21 July 1940 to 27 October 1945) had both executive

---

[VIII] After his abdication, Edvard Beneš retired in his residence in Sezimovo Ústí, and withdrew from public life. On October 18, 1938, he accepted a guest professorship position at the University of Chicago, and left the country rather hurriedly on October 22. After a meeting with President Roosevelt on May 28, 1939 in which Beneš "appeared to receive indications of unofficial support and solidarity", Beneš left for London in beginning of July 1939. In London, he placed himself in head of anti-Nazi resistance movement and formed the exile government. Štefan Osuský was forced out of the exile government because he refused to acknowledge legal continuity of Beneš's presidency. After his abdication, he was not elected by anyone, and his claim for presidency was based solely on the meeting with Roosevelt. Recognition of the exile government by the British was rooted in Churchill's opposition against the Munich Pact (W Curtiss: Manufacturing legitimacy. The Czechoslovak exile government 1938-48).

and legislative powers as the 1920 Constitution did not consider a situation which occurred by creation of the Protectorate. The **Constitution 1920** was defined as poly-legal, what means that it also included acts which were defined as part of the Constitution; and also later incorporated the 15 presidential decrees of Edvard Beneš issued during the period of "non-freedom" which was defined as commencing on September 30, 1938 lasting until May 4, 1945. During this period, the President issued 15 Constitutional Decrees which retrospectively became Constitutional Acts through the **Act 57/1946**. The 1920 Constitution was formally valid until May 1948 when it was replaced by the Gottwald's one.

1.1.4   Soviet influence

The **Czech-Russian Agreement,**[30, 31] (12 December 1943[IX]), The **Czech-Russian Agreement on future jurisdiction on liberated territories**[32] (8 May 1944) and the **Košice Government Program**[33] (5 April 1945) are not formally Constitutional Acts but the nature of these documents significantly affected constitutional development of Czechoslovakia. Former U.S. Ambassador to Czechoslovakia Laurence A Steinhardt in his analysis "Background to the Czechoslovak crisis" for Secretary of State Marshall stated the Czech-Russian Agreement from 1943 a root cause of the constitutional crisis of 1948[34]. In essence, the early post-war presidential decrees of Edvard Beneš only implemented the objectives as defined in the Czech-Russian Agreement and the Košice Government Program. This included orientation of foreign policy towards Slavic nations led by the USSR, exclusion of "fascist elements" from society to protect "the people"; draconian measures against "traitors"; introduction of Peoples' Tribunals, National Committees, and Agrarian Commissions; creation of the National Land Fund for the redistribution of confiscated land; and imposition of the national management over the property of collaborators and traitors and expelled Germans and Hungarians.

In fact, from the timing of the **Teheran Conference**[35] (December 1, 1943), where it was agreed to open the Western Front, and consequent meeting of Stalin with Beneš in Moscow (December 11-12, 1943), it looks more like Stalin's effort to secure resources for operations on the Eastern

---

[IX] There were two significant agreements signed by Czechoslovaks in December 1943. Whilst textbooks of history remain silent about the one signed in Moscow, we learn about so-called "Christmas Agreement" signed between Slovak communists (Husák, Novomeský, Šmidke) and democrats (Ursíny, Lettrich).

Front, whilst using large numbers of both Eastern European[X] and Western European civilians[XI] held hostage in Soviet-controlled territories.

In this context, the outcomes from the **Yalta Conference**[36, 37] can be seen as mere confirmation of deals which were already signed by the Czechoslovak government in exile and not as "Western betrayal" of Eastern European nations. Moreover, as stated above, large numbers of displaced civilians and Allied POWs held by the Red Army in Soviet zone were used by Stalin as leverage during negotiations over recognition of the Polish puppet government of National Unity. It has to be remembered that F.D. Roosevelt suddenly died on April 12, 1945, and there was a transition of power after 12 years in the office to Harry Truman, who was previously not involved in state affairs at this level.

Agreements from **Yalta** discussed repatriation of POWs[38]. Although the agreements from **Potsdam** (July 16, 1945 to August 2, 1945) did approve transfer of displaced civilians, this was supposed to be conducted in an orderly and humane manner[39, 40]. Five days after V-E Day, 200.000 British and 75.000 U.S. soldiers were still held hostage by the Soviet Union in POW camps on Soviet territory. In total, 20.000 U.S. POW and MIAs were never repatriated from various POW camps; 12.500 of these were held hostage by the Red Army in the Soviet zone. Stalin kept them for slave labor and as a tool for blackmail[41].

1.1.5   The Communist coup

The **Constitution from May 1948**[42] formally implemented some objectives as defined in the **Košice Government Program**; but did not legally introduce communist rule in Czechoslovakia. The document does

---

[X] Czechoslovaks who escaped from Protectorate to the USSR were first held in GULAGs, before they were allowed to join Czechoslovak units under Soviet leadership.

[XI] "Latest available displaced persons and prisoners of war figures show almost 1,600,000 Western European (French, Belgian, Dutch and Luxembourgers) either repatriated from or at present held in SHAEF area. Soviet delegates at LEIPZIG conference stated only 300,000 Western Europeans in their area. Combined working party on European food supplies, composed of representatives from UNRRA, SHAEF, USSR, UK, and USA, including Soviet delegate LIUSHENKO, estimated approximately 3,000,000 displaced Western Europeans in enemy-held territory at beginning 1944. This discrepancy of over 100,000 Western Europeans is causing Dutch and French Governments considerable anxiety." (Darby's Rangers, Our 20.000 missing POWs from WW2).

not mention the Communist Party of Czechoslovakia or any other Communist Party (e.g. that of Soviet Union) as a supreme organ of state power. When referring to the origin of the power of the state, it only states "the people". The Constitution directly restricts many fundamental rights as they are defined in the American and French Constitution, documents which inspired the first 1920 Constitution of Czechoslovakia; and also refers to restrictions of some fundamental rights by laws, which already existed at that time, or were supposed to be implemented in the future. The power is formally divided into executive (President and government), legislative (300 members of the National Assembly and 100 members of the Slovakian National Council), and judicial branch (professional and laic judges). Administrative power, although not mentioned in the fundamental articles, is represented by National Committees. Section on economic system defines national, private, and personal property, and directly implements the Košice Government Program from April 1945.

1.1.6   When socialism wins

In July 1960, the new **Constitution 1960**[43] (Act 100/1960) prepared by Pavel Rychetský a Zdeněk Jičínský and signed by Novotný, Fierlinger, and Široký, declared in its introductory essay that socialism won; and formally acknowledged leading role of the Communist Party. Czechoslovak Socialist Republic became a "socialist state based on firm partnership (fasces)[XII] of workers, peasants, and intelligentsia". This Constitution is formed by a long list of political proclamations, and references to the leading role of the Communist Party at all levels of social, economic, and political life. The exact role of the Communist party in the mechanism of power is not specified, though. Its influence was considered ubiquitous, and that's what it was in reality. Socialistic economic system was based on state and cooperative form of ownership, and on 5-year central economic planning. Mandate of members of the National Assembly was shortened to 4 years and presidential functional term to 5 years. This Constitution also introduced function of members of the National Committees who were now formally elected for 4 years, as

---

[XII] This statement can be understood only as a reference to the term "fasces", what as per the Concise Oxford Dictionary means "a bundle of rods with a projecting axe blade, carried by a lector in ancient Rome as a symbol of magistrate power and used as an emblem of authority in fascist Italy".

the way how they occurred in practice was not specified in detail in the 1948 Constitution.

1.1.7   Conscience revisited

The Czech **Constitution 1992**[44], passed after the so called "Velvet divorce" when Czechoslovakia was peacefully divided in two states, brought substantial change; among the most important things it introduced a Declaration of Human Rights and Freedoms as part of the Constitution[XIII]. Political system is based on free competition of political parties which reject violence as tactics how to achieve their objectives. International agreements ratified by Parliament are superior to national laws. Legislative power belongs to Parliament which consists of two chambers – the House with 200 members elected for 4 years, and the Senate, with 81 Senators elected for 6 years. The oath has changed to the promise of loyalty to the Czech Republic, its Constitution and laws, and their own conscience. Executive power comprises of the office of a President and the government; and the judicial branch of Constitutional, Supreme, Supreme Administrative, Highest, Regional, and District Courts. Other institutions introduced in this Constitution are the Highest Bureau for Control, and the Czech National Bank.

1.2   Observations on constitutional development of Czechoslovakia

1.2.1   Between the Wars

The origins of Czechoslovakian national state[XIV] are in the multinational Austrian-Hungarian Empire, and can be traced back to the beginning of the WW1, in which national forces fought on both sides of

---

[XIII] Changes to Constitutions implemented immediately after the fall of communism in Czechoslovakia which eventually resulted in brand new Constitution are described in detail in the paper by Ján Čarnogurský: "The Fall of Communism in Czechoslovakia" http://www.dovekvtisni.cz/download/pdf/static/chapter4.pdf [accessed October 15, 2011]

[XIV] Key role of Czechoslovak intelligence organization Maffia is summarized in Příběh revoluce (The story of revolution) by František Rozhoň, whose main sources were Paměti (Memoirs) by Dr Alois Rašín and Osudové okamžiky Československa (Fateful moments in Czechoslovak history) by Karel Pacner. Full text of this book is available at website Svědomí (Conscience):
http://www.svedomi.cz/pribehy/rof_ceskoslovensko_pribeh_revoluce.htm#r_maffi epripravilavskutkusametovourevoluci [accessed October 13, 2011]

the conflict: the majority remained loyal to the Empire and a minority joined newly forming Czechoslovak legions and fought for a new, national state. After the war, this minority of legionnaires was treated by the new establishment with more respect than the other group, formerly loyal to the Empire, and got priority access to public service. Nevertheless, in 1920, the Constitution of Czechoslovakia was passed and stayed valid until 1948. The most important democratic shortcomings in the pre-WW2 period are not in the formal setup, but in the fact that large groups of the population of the state felt excluded from political life (in violation of the **condition of inclusive citizenship**). The informal coalition agreement among political parties called Pětka, as explained by Frantisek Peroutka[XV], did not help things, either.

Another point would be that the terms for elected officials were a little bit too long (6 years for the House, 8 years for the Senate, and 7 years for the President), what is a consequence of a problem the founding fathers were aware of at that time, and it is missing **talent pool**. If it was not for the geopolitical situation, and the British policy of appeasement in the face of German violation of the Versailles Agreements, the development might have been very different, because new generation of leaders would have had time to grow up. Sadly, during the period pre-WW2 period, there are signs of suppression of new potential players by the very people who were supposed to develop them. Premature death of Milan Rastislav Štefánik in the air crash in 1919[45], and character assassination of Radola Gajda[XVI] contributed to the loss of potential serious players on Czechoslovak political scene.

One of the key conditions of functional democracy, associational autonomy, was abused by neighboring state to profound **subversion** of the state by inflicting conflicts and spreading of violence. The situation

---

[XV] Ferdinand Peroutka on political life in CSR and Pětka in the 1920's in weekly Přítomnost and daily Lidové noviny. Pětka was informal coalition of political parties across Parliament (Agrarians, Social Democracy, National Democrats, Socialist Party, and the Peoples' Party). Main protagonists were Rudolf Bechyně, Antonin Švehla, Alois Rašín, Jan Šrámek and Jiří Stříbrný. R. Kvaček, J. Kuklík, H. Mandelová, I. Pařízková: "XX. Století o sobě. Dějiny v dokumentech;" Dialog 2005.

[XVI] The case of Radola Gajda. Gajda was arrested in 1945, badly tortured in prison, and died of his injuries in 1948. His exclusion from political life was based on serious disagreements with T.G. Masaryk. Frantisek August, Jan Beneš: Ve znamení temna: sovětská špionážní a podvratná činnost proti Československu v letech 1918-1969; pages 34-48. Votobia, 2001 (original: Indiana University).

with the Sudeten-German minority in pre-WW2 Czechoslovakia is frequently compared to current development in Israel and the Gaza strip[46]. Benjamin Netanyahu in his essay Lessons from the Sudetenland[47] explained the importance of Sudeten borderland region for effective defense of the state because of its natural barriers and fortification systems.

The key problem which directly led to the constitutional crisis in Czechoslovakia 1938 and 1939 is reluctance and inability of European leaders, namely the **British policy of appeasement**[XVII], to face the Nazi threat. If there was at least some support from abroad, and expressed determination to assist in the case of escalation of political situation into direct conflict, Czechoslovak leaders would very likely consider different solution[XVIII]. This lack of support of Britain and France to Czechoslovakia, and signing of the Munich Pact with the aggressor instead of providing military assistance, was analyzed in detail in the work of George A Finch: The Nuremberg Trial and International Law[48].

1.2.2   Protectorate and exile government

Hypothetical question what a different leader would have done in this situation, and whether the historical events would unfold in a different way if President Beneš first did not step down after the Munich crisis, and if Hacha did not submit to force in the situation of betrayal by

---

XVII "Judgment of His Majesty's Government, if he might be allowed to state the problem quite crudely, that the result of their combined military and political examination of the issues at stake was that, if the German Government decided to take hostile steps against the Czechoslovak State, it would be impossible, in our present military situation, to prevent those steps from achieving immediate success." (...) "His Majesty's Government regarded it as essential that both Governments should agree that **every effort should be made by Dr. Beneš to reach a settlement of the German minority problem in Czechoslovakia in negotiations with representatives of that minority,"** and that both His Majesty's Government and the French Government should use all their influence, preferably jointly, to further such a settlement. He regarded it as essential that such a settlement should be reached in direct negotiations with Herr Henlein's party." (Lord Halifax on Czechoslovakia, third meeting on **April 29, 1938**; CAB 24/276, National Archives, Kew Gardens).

XVIII Munich Pact could hardly be considered a surprise, though: "Secondly, it should be made very clear to the Czechoslovak Government and to Dr. Beneš that they must seize this opportunity, which might be the last, to make a supreme effort to reach a settlement on this question (Sudeten German minority)." (Ibid)

allies; or if there were different persons in their shoes at that time, nicely relates to the current popular topic of **neuroscience**[XIX] and critical incident decision making. The question is what different people do if systematically bullied[49] out of existence, or when asked to make an uncomfortable decision[50]; and the high science which tries to define under the veil of forensic psychology[51, 52] how much force is required to kick someone into submission. Some methods of psychological coercion as used during the WW2 are explained in graphic detail[XX] in the Authorized history of MI5 Defend the Realm by Christopher Andrew[53], and in the NDIC material Interrogation, WW2, Vietnam, Iraq[54]. In this context, it is irrelevant to think what someone else would do, as person who would have tried to resist the pressure would be likely dead or under arrest anyway, and the political situation would only result into a different type of constitutional crisis with very similar outcome.

The **behavior of a key leader** in a crisis situation does have substantial impact on the morale of the population and international response, though. This can be explained on the case of annexation of Baltic States[55] by Soviet Union, where the Soviets had no choice but to use brute force, instead of completing annexation of Lithuania in a constitutional way, because President Smetona left the country. The fact that the Lithuanian representation did not sign an agreement with the aggressor legally justified the activities of national resistance[56], and also

---

[XIX] "Brander quoted British General Sir Michael Jackson, who said, "Fighting battles is not about territory; it is about people, attitudes, and perceptions. The battleground is there." The book is about testing methods in defense context, and lot of attention is paid to prediction of behavior of key individuals and groups. In this sense, the assumption that "Czechoslovakian leaders will chose not to fight if subjected to pressure" was a correct one, and paid off in easy territory gain. Robert Pool, Rapporteur; Planning Committee on Field Evaluation of Behavioral and Cognitive Sciences-Based Methods and Tools for Intelligence and Counterintelligence: Field Evaluation in the Intelligence and Counterintelligence Context: Workshop Summary; National Research Council, National Academies Press, 2010. http://www.nap.edu/catalog/12854.html [accessed October 13, 2011]

[XX] Methods of R Stephens "Tin Eye" (Camp 020) were based on psychological coercion, sleep deprivation, and disorientation of the prisoner. Although he did not use physical violence, the methods he was using led to nervous breakdowns and suicides. Calder Walton: Torture and intelligence gathering in Western democracies. http://www.historyandpolicy.org/papers/policy-paper-78.html [accessed October 13, 2011]

provided legal grounds for later non-recognition of the annexation of Baltic States by the USA based on the Stimson Doctrine[57].

The situation which occurred after the infamous Hácha's signature was not considered in the 1920 Constitution, and what followed is from constitutional point of view pure improvisation. Looking at the situation from distance, the way of thinking of Hácha and Beneš is strikingly similar. The only difference is that Hácha signed a consent under duress on establishment of Protectorate, whilst trying to correct the damage through domestic resistance later on; and Beneš first abdicated and reinstated himself in power abroad, after removing himself from the power base.

The geopolitical Great Game[58] of **parceling Europe** between two totalitarian regimes in the case of Czechoslovakia materialized already in the Czech-Russian Agreement (December 12, 1943). With regards to the Yalta agreements (February 1945), this in the case of Czechoslovakia only confirmed what was already in place. The Košice Government Program (Apr 1945) then implemented what everybody agreed on (see Soviet influence).

From constitutional development perspective, the 1920 Constitution remained formally valid until May 1948, when it was replaced by the Gottwald's one, but in reality, this document was obsolete since 1938, as it was not enforceable.

The **constitutional vacuum** after the war allowed the interim government to rule through presidential decrees for the crucial period needed to dispose of all potential opposition under the excuse of repatriation of displaced civilians[XXI]. The most violent stage of

---

[XXI] The National Archives Kew Garden: documents of the Foreign Office relating to the Yalta Conference (FO 371/47896). The expulsions started long before Potsdam, and were based on the agreements from Yalta – repatriation of POWs. Ethnic German civilians, who were citizens of Poland (or Czechoslovakia), would not qualify as POWs (Crimea) or displaced civilians (Potsdam), and their mass expulsion was conducted in violation of the Yalta and Potsdam agreements. Potsdam conference legalized their expulsion retrospectively, only demanding the transfer of population to be conducted in "orderly and human manner", but with no enforcement. There are numerous diplomatic notes in the NA archive in Kew Garden regarding this. The documents clearly show distress and fear that the Soviets won't allow people trapped in the Soviet zone to return back to the West. At this time, some anti-Bolshevik Russian nationals were forced to return to USSR (and many committed suicide because they already had experience with Soviet persecution). Comprehensive implementation of communist rule was not launched after the communist coup (Feb 1948), but already after the Košice Government Program (Apr 1945)[59, 60]. As apparent from the Cabinet paper "Threat to Western Civilization"[61], which was circulated within the UK Cabinet in March 1948 as a top secret document, the gravity of the situation was correctly recognized and well understood at that time.

The dynamic of communist takeover in Czechoslovakia was the same as in all other communist regimes, and included mass killings and mass expulsions (as an alternative to mass killings) in the first stage; then mass arrests, show trials, and the use of judicial system as demonstration of force in the second stage; and eventually economic incentives and security apparatus when the regime became more stable[62].

The constitutional vacuum between 1945 and 1948 was one the key conditions of the violent first stage, when the perpetrators engaged in mass atrocities under the promise of impunity.

1.2.3 Building the bright future

The 1948 Constitution and Constitutional and other Acts which followed retrospectively legalized acts of National Committees which would otherwise be unlawful[63, 64], and launched the second stage of implementation of communist regime, in which the state formally, even though not in practice, followed its own regulations. Most of the violence of the state against the population is then performed through its judicial and police system[65].

The 1960 Constitution stated that "socialism won", what moved the regime in its third stage. This process can be compared to the 13th century Mongol way of taming a wild horse. The horse understands that there is no point fighting the ropes, as it only causes more pain and anguish, and eventually after a period of fierce struggle submits to the rider. After this stage, it is no longer needed to rely on brute force, as the horse already knows what happens in case of disobedience. The harness is on and the horse cannot remove it. To the frustration of the conqueror, some horses fail to acknowledge the authority of the rider despite being in severe pain; what leads to unnecessary injuries and accusations of the concerned riders that certain borrowed or stolen wild ponies have learning

---

summary of selected correspondence is available at Darby's Rangers web (Our 20.000 missing POWs of WW2).

disabilities or are too aggressive to be handled[66]. From this point of view, the Prague spring, invasion, and the reprisals which followed can be seen as revolt which had no chance to succeed, but allowed the rulers to identify rebellious characters. These were then neutralized in the normalization period[67].

Once implemented, totalitarian regimes are relatively stable, and their biggest problem is in economic inefficiency[68], which stems from systematic liquidation of human capital. Communist Czechoslovakia based its economic development on looting resources[69] and expansion[70]. Periodically, people were allowed to accumulate property, which was in next stage collected and redistributed to a chosen (in this case communist) minority[XXII]. Economic pressure was used by the regime as a way of keeping people in submission, as lack of resources for anything but basic survival made effective resistance to the regime impossible.

King Banaian in his work Demand for democide[71] analyzes correlation between the numbers of people killed by government and property rights, and asks whether the main factor for non-violence is in fact democracy or property rights. This is a very interesting question, because I cannot imagine a democratic government which would not respect property rights equally in all its subjects, or an authoritarian government which would respect any rights, including property rights, equally. These two factors are closely related, and what might be needed is better definition of democracy and authoritarian regime.

XXII As stated by Richard Pipes in his study of Struve, there is no political freedom without economic independence. Liquidation of economic backbone of the state started by expulsion of Sudeten Germans in 1945, then continued by collectivization of farms, monetary reform in 1953, confiscation and nationalization of private property from large industries to small businesses, forced evictions as part of Action Bourgeoisie, and formation of forced labor camps, uranium mining based on slave labor, in a desperate attempt to compensate self-inflicted destruction of economic powerbase.

References:

1 Hitler's Decree 75/1939 on the establishment of Protectorate Böhmen und Mahren. Full text of this decree is available in Czech at Fronta.cz http://www.fronta.cz/dokument/hitleruv-vynos-o-zrizeni-protektoratu-cechy-a-morava [accessed October 12, 2011]

2 Curtiss W: Manufacturing legitimacy: The Czechoslovak Exile Government, 1938-1945. Williamson College, Williamstown, Massachusetts, April 16 2007. http://library.williams.edu/theses/pdf.php?id=185 [accessed Oct 10 2011]

3 Constitutional crisis created by the establishment of Protectorate. Ústavní vývoj Československý v roce 1938: Part II – Otázka formální kontinuity mezi právním stavem, přivoděným zářijovými a říjnovými událostmi roku 1938 a stavem dřívějším. Available in Czech at Fronta.cz http://www.fronta.cz/dokument/ustavni-vyvoj-ceskoslovensky-v-roce-1938-cast-ii [accessed October 12, 2011]

4 Abdication speech of Edvard Beneš from October 5, 1938. Full text of transcript of this speech is available at Fronta.cz http://www.fronta.cz/dokument/edvard-benes-posledni-rozhlasovy-projev-5-rijna-1938 [accessed October 12, 2011]

5 Mlsna P, Šlehofer L, Urban D: The paths of Czech Constitutionality. On the 90th anniversary of the passage of the first Czechoslovak constitution. Page 75. The document is bilingual, available in both Czech and English. Government Office, 2010. http://www.vlada.cz/assets/udalosti/vystavy/Cesty-ceske-ustavnosti.pdf [accessed October 12, 2011]

6 Constitutional Act 57/1946 from March 28, 1946, which approved all decrees issued by President Beneš and proclaimed them Acts. Parliament of the Czech Republic. http://www.psp.cz/docs/laws/dek/u1946.html [accessed October 12, 2011]

7 Munich Pact from September 29, 1938, signed by Adolf Hitler (Nazi Germany), Neville Chamberlain (Great Britain), Edouard Daladier (France), and Benito Mussolini (Italy): English translation is available at the Yale Law School, Lillian Goldman Law Library, The Avalon Project: http://avalon.law.yale.edu/imt/munich1.asp [accessed October 12, 2011]; Scanned original of the Munich Agreement in German is available at blog of Jiří Kučera: http://jirikkucera.files.wordpress.com/2011/03/mc3bcnchner-abkommen1.pdf [accessed October 12, 2011]

8 Nuremberg Trial Proceedings, Volume 22: Judgement of the Nuremberg Tribunal from September 30, 1946; Yale Law School; Lillian Goldman law Library; The Avalon Project. http://avalon.law.yale.edu/imt/09-30-46.asp [accessed October 12, 2011]

9 ILO: 70th Anniversary of the Infamous Munich Agreement. International Law Observer http://internationallawobserver.eu/2008/09/28/70th-anniversary-of-the-infamous-munich-agreement/ [accessed October 12, 2011]

10 Finch George A: The Nuremberg Trial and International Law. Vol 41, No 1 (Jan 1947); 20-37. Part relating to the Munich Agreement: pages 26-27. Available at http://www.st-andrews.ac.uk/itsold/papers/public/miscellaneous/printingproblems/nurem.pdf [accessed 30 May 2011]

11 The British Constitution: There is no single document codified as Constitution. History Learning Site. http://www.historylearningsite.co.uk/british_constitution.htm [accessed October 12, 2011]

12 The British Constitution and Monarchy. Public affairs for journalists 2009; Online Resource Centre: "For any state to achieve a sense of order and identity, it requires a shared set of values to be recognized and accepted by its subjects." Full text of the document is available at

http://www.oup.com/uk/orc/bin/9780199552610/morrison_ch01.pdf [accessed October 12, 2011]

13 Walker A: Nazi War Trials. Pocket Essentials Series; November 2005.

14 Phillips, John T., II: George Washington's Rules of Civility: Complete With the Original French Text and New French-To-English Translations (The Complete George Washington Series, Vol. 1); Goose Creek Productions; Collector's edition; November 30, 2003.

15 Committee on Science, Engineering, and Public Policy: On Being a Scientist: A Guide to Responsible Conduct in Research. National Academy of Sciences, National Academy of Engineering, and Institute of Medicine, 2009. http://www.nap.edu/catalog/12192.html [accessed October 12, 2011]

16 The Cleveland agreement (signed on October 22, 1915) as commented in: R. Kvaček, J. Kuklík, H. Mandelová, I. Pařízková: "XX. Století o sobě. Dějiny v dokumentech;" Dialog 2005. The agreement is cited at http://www.moderni-dejiny.cz/danek-clevelandska-dohoda-22-23-10-1915-108/ [accessed October 12, 2011]

17 The Pittsburgh Agreement (signed on May 30, 1918) as commented in: R. Kvaček, J. Kuklík, H. Mandelová, I.Pařízková: "XX. Století o sobě. Dějiny v dokumentech;" Dialog 2005. The agreement itself is cited at the web of Waymarking, under post The 1918 Pittsburgh Agreement – M.R. Štefánik memorial, Bratislava, Slovakia. http://www.waymarking.com/waymarks/WMAZPN_The_1918_Pittsburgh_Agreement_MRStefanik_memorial_Bratislava_Slovakia. [accessed October 12, 2011]

18 The Washington Declaration as cited in: R. Kvaček, J. Kuklík, H. Mandelová, I. Pařízková: "XX. Století o sobě. Dějiny v dokumentech;" Dialog 2005. Czechoslovakia accepted the ideals of modern democracy on American principles as defined in the Declaration of Independence and the Bill of Rights. Full text of the Agreement is cited on the webpage of Petr Just http://www.just.wz.cz/view.php?cislodanku=2006071303 [accessed October 12, 2011]

19 Recognition of Czechoslovakia as in independent state, codified in the Saint Germain-en-Laye Agreement from September 10, 1919; published in: R. Kvaček, J. Kuklík, H. Mandelová, I. Pařízková: "XX. Století o sobě. Dějiny v dokumentech;" Dialog 2005. Available at Naval History: http://navalhistory.flixco.info/H/181013/8330/a0.htm - The Covenant of the League of Nations. [accessed October 12, 2011]. Full text of the Treaty is available here (section III, Articles 53-58): http://www.austlii.edu.au/au/other/dfat/treaties/1920/3.html [accessed October 12, 2011]

20 The Philadelphian Agreement as published in: R. Kvaček, J. Kuklík, H. Mandelová, I.Pařízková: "XX. Století o sobě. Dějiny v dokumentech;" Dialog 2005.

21 The Martin Declaration as published in: R. Kvaček, J. Kuklík, H. Mandelová, I. Pařízková: "XX. Století o sobě. Dějiny v dokumentech;" Dialog 2005.

22 Bakke Elisabeth: The Autonomy discourse in Parliamentary debates during the first Czechoslovak Republic and after the Velvet Revolution. Department of Political Science, University of Oslo. Published in the scholarly annual Slovakia (Vol XXXVII), numbers 70-71, 2005. (Slovak League of America) http://folk.uio.no/stveb1/Autonomy_discourse.pdf [accessed October 12, 2011]

23 Library of Congress: Early history of Czechoslovakia. http://www.loc.gov/rr/european/imsk/slovakia.html [accessed October 12, 2011]

24 The Interim Constitution from 1918 as published on the web of Czech Parliament. Act 37/1918, full text available at: http://www.psp.cz/docs/texts/constitution_1918.html [accessed October 12, 2011]

25 Current Swiss constitution. http://www.admin.ch/ch/e/rs/1/101.en.pdf [accessed October 12, 2011]. History of Switzerland: Switzerland's way towards the federal constitution of 1848. The Federal constitution of 1848 combines elements of the U.S. constitution and of French revolutionary tradition. http://history-switzerland.geschichte-schweiz.ch/switzerland-federal-constitution-1848.html [October 12, 2011]

26 The Constitution from 1920; web of the Czech Parliament: Constitutional Act 121/1920. http://www.psp.cz/docs/texts/constitution_1920.html [accessed October 12, 2011]

27 Constitution of the United States of America. My Hillsdale College copy which I have got from Jan Beneš. Otherwise at http://www.usconstitution.net/const.html [accessed on October 12, 2011]

28 The Constitution of the Austrian-Hungarian Empire from 1867. Available at http://cs.wikipedia.org/wiki/Prosincov%C3%A1_%C3%BAstava [accessed October 12, 2011]

29 Constitution of the Third French Republic. http://www.assemblee-nationale.fr/histoire/constitution-troisieme-republique.asp [accessed October 12, 2011]

30 Edvard Beneš's Chancellor Jaromír Smutný in his personal notes from visit of President Beneš in Moscow December 11 to 12, 1943 described negotiations of Czech representation with Stalin. The participants representing the Czech side were Gottwald, Nejedlý, Smutný, and Beneš. Soviet side was represented by J.V. Stalin, M.I. Kalinin, I.M. Majskij, A.M. Vasilevskij, and K.J. Vorošilov. Molotov was assisting Beneš with translations, as Beneš's Russian was not good enough to be able to discuss the matters without an interpreter. Published in: R. Kvaček, J. Kuklík, H. Mandelová, I. Pařízková: "XX. Století o sobě. Dějiny v dokumentech;" Dialog 2005.

31 Treaty on friendship, mutual assistance, and post-war cooperation between Czechoslovak Republic and the USSR signed in Moscow on December 12, 1943. The agreement was published in February 1946 by a Notice of the Ministry of Interior, and is cited in Appendix.

32 Agreement concerning the relationship between the Czechoslovak government and the Soviet Commander in Chief on the entry of Soviet troops into Czechoslovak territory. The treaty was signed by Minister of Foreign Affairs and a State Minister Hubert Ripka, who was entitled to act on behalf of the Czechoslovak exile government, with Ambassador extraordinary and plenipotentiary of the USSR to the government of the Czechoslovak Republic V. Lebedev on May 8, 1944, in London. The treaty was obtained in Czech and English versions from the National Archive in Prague, fund NUKU-L, box No 18; and is cited in Appendix.

33 The Košice Government Program from April 5, 1945. Full text in Czech: http://www.svedomi.cz/dokdoby/1945_kosvlpr.htm [accessed October 12, 2011]; Summary in English: http://www.anticomm.co.uk/?p=295 [accessed October 12, 2011]

34 Attitude of the United States with respect to the Czechoslovak governmental crisis of February 1948 and its aftermath. On April 30, 1948, former U.S. Ambassador in CSR Laurence Steinhardt sent a detailed analysis of the situation in Czechoslovakia "Background to the Czechoslovak Crisis" to the Secretary of State Marshall. This analysis is cited in full in Appendix. The memorandums are available online at http://images.library.wisc.edu/FRUS/EFacs/1948v04/reference/frus.frus1948v04.i0 007.pdf [accessed on October 12, 2011]

35 "Military conclusions of the Tehran conference: (4) Took note that Operation OVERLORD would be launched during May 1944, in conjunction with an operation against Southern France. The latter operation would be undertaken in as great a strength as availability of landing-craft permitted. The Conference further took note of Marshal Stalin's statement that the Soviet forces would launch an offensive at about the same time with the object of preventing the German forces from transferring from the Eastern to the Western Front." Teheran Conference, November 28 to December 1, 1943. The Avalon Project, Yale Law School: http://www.yale.edu/lawweb/avalon/wwii/tehran.htm [accessed October 14, 2011]

36 Yale Law School, Lillian Goldman Library, The Avalon Project; Article XII: http://avalon.law.yale.edu/20th_century/decade17.asp [accessed October 12, 2011]

37 The Yalta Conference: The Big Three during the War:

http://www.johnddare.net/cold_war4.htm [accessed October 13, 2011]

38 The Yalta Conference: National Archives Kew Garden: FO 371/47896. Agreements concerning prisoners of war and civilians liberated by forces operating under United States Command: Crimea (Yalta) 11 Feb 1945. United States interpretation of provisions N3457/409/38.
http://yourarchives.nationalarchives.gov.uk/index.php?title=Yalta_Conference_in_t he_Crimea_between_the_Soviet_Union%2C_UK_and_US%2C_1945 [accessed October 12, 2011]

39 Potsdam Conference (July 16, 1945 to August 2, 1945: Department of the Navy – Naval Historical Center. Online library of selected images. World War II Diplomacy: http://www.history.navy.mil/photos/events/wwii-dpl/hd-state/potsdam.htm [accessed October 12, 2011]

40 Student Activity: Harry Truman and the Potsdam Conference. The Truman Library http://www.trumanlibrary.org/teacher/potsdam.htm [accessed October 12, 2011]

41 Darby's Rangers: WWII's 20.000 MIA. Our missing POWs of WWII. http://darbysrangers.tripod.com/id67.htm [accessed October 13, 2011]

42 Constitution of May 1948. Constitutional Act 150/1948 (May 9, 1948). Available at web of Czech Parliament: http://www.psp.cz/docs/texts/constitution_1948.html [accessed October 13, 2011]

43 Constitution of July 1960. Constitutional Act 100/1960 (July 11, 1960). Available at web of Czech Parliament: http://www.psp.cz/docs/texts/constitution_1960.html [accessed October 13]

44 Constitution of 1992. Constitutional Act 1/1993 (December 1992). Available at the web of Czech Parliament. http://www.psp.cz/docs/laws/constitution.html [accessed October 12, 2011]

45 Simon TF: Milan Rastislav Štefánik. MR Štefánik died in an air crash on May 4, 1919. http://www.tfsimon.com/stefanik-note.htm [accessed October 13, 2011]

46 Salpeter E: Sudeten Germans continue fight for right of return. Haaretz, September 3, 2003. Available at Haaretz: http://www.haaretz.com/print-edition/features/sudeten-germans-continue-fight-for-right-of-return-1.98974 [accessed October 13, 2011]

47 Netanjahu B: Lessons from the Sudetenland. Koinonia House, http://www.khouse.org/articles/1997/11/ [accessed October 13, 2011].

48 Finch George A: The Nuremberg Trial and International Law. Vol 41, No 1 (Jan 1947); 20-37. Available at St. Andrews: .http://www.st-andrews.ac.uk/itsold/papers/public/miscellaneous/printingproblems/nurem.pdf [accessed October 13, 2011]

49 Hanson S, Davis M, Altevogt B, Rapporteur; Forum on Neuroscience and Nervous System Disorders: CNS Clinical Trials: Suicidality and Data Collection:

Workshop Summary. National Academies Press, page 22, Figure 2-1; 2010. http://www.nap.edu/catalog/12829.html [accessed October 13, 2011]

50 Bradley, CP: Uncomfortable prescribing decisions: a critical incident study. British Medical Journal 1992; Volume 304:294-6. "Incidents are deemed to be critical when the purpose of the action and the outcome of the incident are reasonably clear and relevant to the phenomenon under study", in other words, which doctors are more happy than others not to treat the patient to the best of his or her ability. http://www.ncbi.nlm.nih.gov/pmc/articles/PMC1881047/pdf/bmj00058-0034.pdf [accessed October 13, 2011]

51 University of Liverpool: Centre for Critical & Major Incident Psychology. http://www.liv.ac.uk/psychology/ccir/ [accessed October 13, 2011]

52 University of Liverpool: MSc 1-year Course Investigative & Forensic Psychology. http://www.liv.ac.uk/psychology/pg/invforpsy.html [accessed October 13, 2011]

53 Andrew C: Defend the Realm: The authorized history of MI5, page 250-253; Knopf 2009. More on Camp 020 can be found in the National Archives, Kew Gardens. http://www.nationalarchives.gov.uk/releases/2007/march/policy.htm [accessed October 13, 2011]

54 National Defense Intelligence College: Interrogation, World War II, Vietnam, and Iraq. NDIC Press 2008. http://www.ndic.edu/press/12010.htm [accessed October 13, 2011]

55 Communist crimes: "On 15-16 June 1940 the Red Army occupied Lithuania. The Soviet troops also occupied parts of southwest Lithuania, which had been ceded to Germany by the Soviet-German treaty of 28 September 1939. The annexation plan was based on the goal of completing Lithuania's annexation by the USSR while formally following the Constitution and laws of Lithuania. This failed due to the departure of Smetona. On 17 June, a new Government, dubbed the People's Government, was formed and approved by Acting President Antanas Merkys." http://www.communistcrimes.org/en/Database/Lithuania/Historical-Overview [accessed October 13, 2011]

56 Beneš J: Zločin genocidy. Votobia 2001.

57 Vitas RA: United States and Lithuania. The Stimson Doctrine of non-recognition. Praeger Publishers, 1990.

58 WW2 behind closed doors. A problem with Poland. Stalin offers British foreign secretary Anthony Eden a secret deal concerning the fate of Poland. December 1941. http://www.pbs.org/behindcloseddoors/episode-1/ep1_problem_with_poland.html [accessed October 13, 2011]

59 Pekárková, K: Mass graves in Ďáblice: Čestné pohřebiště popravených a umučených politických vězňů v Praze-Ďáblicích. (Honorary graveyard of political prisoners who were either executed or tortured to death). They are all dumped in a mass grave together with everything what was found in the area at that time, from armies to local Nazis and deceased civilians.

www.arcig.cz/projekty/historseminar/pekarkova.doc [accessed October 14, 2011]

60 Temné svědectví na Ďáblickém hřbitově. http://www.dablice.cz/?view=39,464,0,0,0,0,39,-1&cat=7 [accessed October 14, 2011]

61 CAB 129/25 Ernest Bevin: The threat to Western Civilisation. Cabinet papers, March 1948. National Archives Kew Garden. Can be downloaded from the National Archives: http://www.nationalarchives.gov.uk/documentsonline/details-result.asp?queryType=1&resultcount=1&Edoc_Id=7970998 [accessed October 14, 2011]

62 Courtois S, Werth N, Panne JL, Paczkowski A, Bartošek K, Margolin JL: Černá kniha komunismu – zločiny, terror, represe I, II. (Black book of communism; Crimes, terror, repressions I, II). Paseka 1999.

63 Act 213/1948 available at Portal.gov.cz: §1, (1) "Measures taken by the Action Committees, on their proposal, or on their behalf in the period between February 20, 1948, to the date when this Act comes in effect, which were directed to securing of the peoples-democratic establishment or cleaning of public life, are considered lawful even in cases where their actions would not otherwise be in line with relevant regulations.http://www.portal.gov.cz/wps/portal/_s.155/701/.cmd/ad/.c/313/.ce/10821/.p/8411/_s.155/701?PC_8411_p=1&PC_8411_l=213/1948&PC_8411_ps=10#10821[accessed October 14, 2011]

64 Act 213/1948, Original as obtained from the Museum of Third Resistance: http://www.anticomm.co.uk/?p=1023 [accessed October 14, 2011]

65 Hejl V: Zpráva o organizovaném násilí (Report on organized violence). Univerzum 1990.

66 Monty Roberts: Shy Boy - the horse who came in from the wild.

67 Valdova V, Zverina P: Case of Jiri Wolf - Personification of Innocence. Available at http://www.anticomm.co.uk/?p=558 [accessed June 4, 2011].

68 Stalin JV: Economic problems of socialism in the USSR. The book was written in 1952, a year before Stalin's death, and published by progressive Party line in 1972 in Beijing after the Sino-Soviet split. Progressive party wing makes a claim that Stalin was in fact murdered because of the analysis of economic situation in the USSR, which was in conflict with ideology. http://www.marx2mao.com/PDFs/EPS52.pdf [accessed October 14, 2011]

69 Pipes R: Russia under the new regime. Penguin Non-classics, 1997. This book contains perfect description of the tsarist cast of "dvorjane" and their transition into the class of "apparatchiks", including all conditions which contributed to this unique economic model.

70 Andrew C, Mitrokhin V: World was going our way. Basic Books 2005. KGB operations in the third world were primarily directed at countries rich in natural resources which would provide strategic leverage (oil, gas, uranium) or easy income

(cheap labor). Perfect examples are Venezuela (oil, base for Bears), Mexico (drug smuggling, production of vast numbers of refugees and poor migrants, what creates a problem for the primary adversary which has not changed since the Cold War), North Korea (used mainly for blackmail, forgery business), Middle East (oil and gas, demographic threat directed against Europe), and Caucasus (excuse for draconian anti-terrorist laws in Russia; oil and gas). Czechoslovakia got involved mainly in Cuba and North Korea. KGB was heavily involved in spreading anti-US conspiracy theories.

71 Banaian K: The Demand for Democide: An Instrumental Variables Analysis. Independent Institute Working Paper Number 43; 2001. http://www.independent.org/pdf/working_papers/43_democide.pdf. [accessed October 14, 2011]

2 KEY POINTS FROM HISTORY

Robert A Dahl in his paper "What institutions does large scale democracy require?" defined six conditions crucial for functional modern polyarchal democracy: elected representation, free, fair, and frequent elections, alternative information, freedom of expression, associational autonomy, and inclusive citizenship. The following section contains some observations of critical incidents from the history of Czechoslovakia, in relation to their impact on its democratic development.

2.1 Straying away from the American-French foundations (1918 to 1945)

The founding documents were inspired by the American and French model and brought to life by T.G. Masaryk, E. Beneš, and R. Štefánik. During this era, the role of Czechoslovak intelligence organization called **Maffia** cannot be underestimated, as it clearly had crucial role in negotiating support for the newly forming state. Following the death of Milan Rastislav Štefánik in an air crash at Bratislava airport in May 1919, Slovak representation lost one of its most important leaders. Radola Gajda[72] had serious disagreements with Masaryk and was excluded from the narrow group of people who make the weather. Already in 1926, Gajda was accused of preparing a coup, and attacked from all sides. His fall helped former Austrian-Hungarian officers who were loyal to the empire to get back in power. Gajda was imprisoned in 1945, badly tortured in prison, and died of his injuries in 1948. One of the most devastating democratic deficits of the First Republic as I can see it is suppression of talent pool, and exclusion of large groups of political opposition from access to state administration and to public service and in many respects were treated as second class citizens.

Although the First Republic was in theory a multinational state, the "Czechoslovak" nation clearly distinguished itself from non-Slavic nations, namely Germans and Hungarians. Sudeten German minority, which formed economic backbone of the state, felt very disgruntled by this status of affairs, and paid back with growing disloyalty. Question remains whether this opposition could have been overcome in the face of growing German nationalism. Failure to build relationships with neighbors (especially Poland) proved to have devastating consequences later on.

Czech presidents are compared to the first one, T.G. Masaryk, who in my opinion stayed in the office way too long, and especially towards the end of his presidency, he failed to address the coming threat of raising Nazism and growing disloyalty of the German minority despite being regularly briefed on this topic by the team of Frantisek Moravec[73].

As a result of missing pool of talents who could later become political leaders, the power was literally handed over to Beneš, and then Hácha, people who were considered "non-threatening" by all; and at the time of a critical incident he failed to do what was needed. Decision he made under pressure essentially sent his nation into slavery, and delegitimized resistance against occupying force; despite having at his disposal one of the best prepared armies in Europe[74], fighting from a high ground[XXIII], and high morale of both the forces and the population. Hácha signed the consent with creation of Protectorate with Hitler, despite being fully aware of the consequences, as he was educated in international law and politics. Those who refused to accept the new situation which followed by the creation of Protectorate were forced to leave the country and join armies of states which were not yet overrun by Nazi Germany. This signature created very difficult situation for those who left the Protectorate and joined foreign armed forces to fight the Nazis. This changed after the exile government joined the war effort on the side of Allies[75]. Legal status of Czechoslovak airmen within the Royal Air Force is described in detail in the study Airmen in exile by Alan Brown[76].

At the same time, the exile government of Edvard Beneš was already negotiating support with a different authoritarian regime. The argument that Beneš was unaware of the realities of Stalin's Russia cannot withstand confrontation with reality, as he was an eye-witness of the Bolshevik revolution during the time he spent with the legions.[XXIV] During the Bolshevik Revolution, when Czechoslovak legionnaires got involved in clashes with Red Guards, Edvard Beneš who was sitting in Paris at that time gave order to hand over arms to the Revolutionary Guards[77]. The

---

XXIII Map of Czechoslovakia: Even though the country neighbors with Germany from nearly ¾ of the length of its border, the barrier of border mountain ranges crate relatively good base for effective defense. Disloyal Sudeten German minority lived exactly in this strategically important territory.

XXIV Masaryk was expelled from Russia and had to leave Russian legions to Beneš. Moreover, Beneš met Stalin during his visit in Moscow in 1935. Ceska Narodni Rada: Armada a narod. Nakladatelství Mazáč 1938.

role of Jaroslav Hašek[78], during WW1 as the chief commissionaire on Russian front, should also be remembered in this context. Edvard Beneš's sympathy for the Soviets can be traced back to his times in Russia in early 1920's[79].

Post-war failure of the Beneš's government to re-establish democracy can be seen as a direct consequence of the agreements signed by the Czechoslovak exile government with the Soviets during the WW2. To answer how is it possible that the Czechoslovak delegation was so badly prepared when negotiating terms with the Soviets in December 1943 is a question for historians.

2.2   Rocky road from national to international socialism (1945 to 1960)

Czechoslovak anti-Nazi resistance, both domestic and foreign, was declared illegal by one stroke of a pen. From this perspective, silent collaboration of the majority of population with the occupying force is perfectly understandable. Frustration from this enforced but not consensual state regime materialized after the war in Czech national fury against the perceived origin of the problem, the German and Hungarian nationals who were used simply as scapegoats; and also more than welcome diversion of public anger from their own elected representation. During spring and summer 1945, Czechoslovakia became a killing ground[xxv, 80].

Post-war development in Czechoslovakia was legally grounded in the presidential decrees issued by the Beneš's government, which kept this unity of executive and legislative power until October 1945. In September 1946, the Nuremberg War Crimes Tribunal declared the Munich Agreement invalid; and in the case of Czechoslovakia formally confirmed

---

[xxv] The total number of casualties during the war, including aftermaths of Operation Anthropoid, was between 100.000 and 130.000, including Jews. From the total pre-war number 118.000, approximately 80.000 died as per the presentation on History of Anti-Semitism on June 2, 2011; source: Jewish museum in Prague; 90.000 Jews or more as per the Survivor's Guide. Very few Czech Jews managed to escape. During the 1.5 year (spring 1945 – before Potsdam! to 1946, most of the killing done before the elections) over 2.5 million were forcibly displaced and 300.000 died in various reprisals. Source: Clayton A Oliver: Survivor's Guide to the Czech Republic. An unofficial setting sourcebook for Twilight 2013. http://web.mac.com/c_oliver/2013/Survivors_Guide_to_the_Czech_Republic.pdf. [accessed October 14, 2011]

the status quo regarding its territorial integrity, and invalidated Nazi territorial gains.

Czechoslovakia had very uneasy relationship with Czech exiles who decided to leave the Nazi occupied state and fight the Nazis under the command of foreign armed forces. This is in direct conflict with the rhetoric of the Beneš government which presented itself as head of anti-Nazi resistance. Graphic example of this seemingly illogical approach is the fate of Czechs who had served in the Royal Air Force[81]. The new Beneš's government could not need people with real combat experience within the state administration, as he clearly considered them a threat. Heroic welcome for RAF airmen expected by many did not materialize. Air Marshall Karel Janousek[82], a person who organized Czechoslovak squadrons within the RAF, was after return removed from all positions of significance and imprisoned. Czechoslovak anti-communist resistance was heavily infiltrated by StB (Svetlana[83, 84, 85], Black Lion 777[86], Masin Brothers[87], Silver Fox[88] group, and many others). The only relatively efficient part was the section which cooperated with American CIC[89].

As agreed at Yalta[90], displaced prisoners of war and civilians were supposed to be repatriated to their country of origin. In Potsdam[XXVI], transfer of ethnic Germans and Hungarians from Poland and Czechoslovakia to Germany was approved, providing the population transfers will be conducted in orderly and humane manner. The only

---

[XXVI] Full text of paragraph XII: "The Three Governments, having considered the question in all its aspects, recognize that the transfer to Germany of German populations, or elements thereof, remaining in Poland, Czechoslovakia and Hungary, will have to be undertaken. They agree that any transfers that take place should be effected in an orderly and humane manner. Since the influx of a large number of Germans into Germany would increase the burden already resting on the occupying authorities, they consider that the Control Council in Germany should in the first instance examine the problem, with special regard to the question of the equitable distribution of these Germans among the several zones of occupation. They are accordingly instructing their respective representatives on the Control Council to report to their Governments as soon as possible the extent to which such persons have already entered Germany from Poland, Czechoslovakia and Hungary, to submit an estimate of the time and rate at which further transfers could be carried out having regard to the present situation in Germany. The Czechoslovak Government, the Polish Provisional Government and the Control Council in Hungary are at the same time being informed of the above and are being requested meanwhile to suspend further expulsions pending an examination by the Governments concerned of the report from their representatives on the Control Council."

international response to violence was at the level of diplomatic notes. By the time of the 1946 elections, the ethnic cleansing and revenge against collaborators and traitors, including major shifts in ownership of the confiscated property, were completed.

Series of purges in all sectors of public life followed after the putsch. Judges and prosecutors were replaced by communists only, and the era of political show trials was launched to create an atmosphere of hopelessness and fear. How many people were slaughtered, imprisoned, forced into exile, or removed from positions of influence during this journey from national to international socialism, is subject to disputes among historians, both professional and amateur[91]. Was far as I can see it, the point of no return was reached already in November 1945, when the Beneš's cabinet felt free to provide Czechoslovak "ore and concentrates containing radium and other radioactive elements" to the Soviets, and sign the so called Uranium Agreement[XXVII] with their representatives. In this secret treaty, Czechoslovakia surrendered its greatest asset and effectively sold its own population for slave labor, hoping nobody will notice.

2.3 Let the dead bury their dead (1960 to 1989)

Constitution of 1960 written by Pavel Rychetský & Zdeněk Jičínský formally implemented victory of socialism, and created firm legal basis for the function of secret services and the police – power structures concentrated under the Ministry of Interior[92]. As the large-scale killing phase of implementation of the regime was already over, this stage is generally considered less brutal. From international context[93], the information brought to the West by Oleg Penkovsky[94] before the Cuban crisis (1962)[95], and others (e.g. Gordievski[96, 97, 98] Mitrokhin[99], Belenko[100]), the only conclusion coming from this can be that the regime simply consolidated power at home and moved on.

In Czechoslovakia, series of pro-Soviet presidents followed, some hard-line, some moderate. The Prague Spring[101] [102] resulted in diplomatic crisis[103] [104] [105] and eventually invasion of Warsaw Pact military[106] [107] The Soviet invasion, perceived by the population as inappropriate use of force,

---

[XXVII] Agreement of the governments of Czechoslovak Republic and the USSR from November 23, 1945, and Protocol on mining of uranium ore in CSR and supplies to the USSR Source: Frantisek Lepka: Czech Uranium. Unknown economical and political context 1945-2002. The treaty is cited in full in Appendix.

led to emigration of 300.000 Czechs and Slovaks and also defection of several high level communists to the West, namely Frolík[108, 109] and Sejna[110, 111]. National amnesia[112] relating to murdered and vanished neighbors, POWs[113, 114], intelligentsia, bourgeoisie, clergy, kulaks, political opposition, business rivals, and all other undesirables, and general acceptance of the communist rule as a fact of life created a strange national mindset, where number of dead simply did not matter anymore, as long as "they" do not touch "us". Everybody understood the rules.

The few, who refused to follow orders during the Soviet invasion in 1968, were immediately reminded of the rules of engagement. Those, who dared to challenge the status quo, were removed from service and the most active ones were sentenced to many years in prison in non-public trials[XXVIII].

Normalization during the 1970's introduced system of carrot and stick, where those who never challenged the status quo and were happy to express selective blindness towards occasional violations of human rights by the state were rewarded by permission to breathe and even make a living. This social contract was in case of need amended by requests to cooperate with local StB[XXIX], and provide the organs with some entirely harmless information necessary to do their dirty work[115]. The negotiating methods used by the StB included the use of compromising material, and threat of loss of income or accommodation, especially in situations when the subject was most vulnerable – typically families with very young children. This way, vast majority of the nation was literally dragged into active collaboration with the regime. Root cause of this

---

XXVIII "The Czechoslovak People's Army, having failed to oppose the Soviet intervention and defend the country's sovereignty, suffered a tremendous loss of prestige after 1968. At Soviet direction, reliable Czechoslovak authorities conducted a purge and political reeducation campaign in the Czechoslovak People's Army and cut its size. With its one-time closest partner now proven unreliable, the Soviet Union turned to Poland as its principal East European ally. Library of Congress: Federal Research Division, Country Studies: http://lcweb2.loc.gov/frd/cs/soviet_union/su_appn.html [accessed October 14, 2011]

XXIX Cibulkovy seznamy (Cibulka's list) contain approximately 600.000 names of co-operators with StB. The list of StB confidents obtained by Petr Cibulka and David Eleder. This number does not include Party members and employees of power ministries, police and the military.

widespread collaboration was economic dependence on predatory state[xxx] as the sole provider of employment and income.

2.4 Brand new world (after 1989)

2.4.1 Privatization

Constitution 1992 once again created various institutions based on western models. After initial shock, economic boom and opening of the borders to the West significantly improved living standards, including medical care and life expectations. Small business thrived and transfer of property in private hands did have positive effect on economic growth. Privatization was a success, despite numerous scandals which were making the headlines during the 1990's to the point when readers got the impression that there is nothing to steal anymore. David Ellerman in his paper "Lessons from voucher privatization" [116] tells different story[xxxi], though, and this analysis seem to resemble reality much closer than idealistic depiction of "East European tiny tigers"[117].

[xxx] This dependence was twofold – not only citizens of satellite countries on their respective governments, but also dependence of economies of satellite states on the Soviet Union: "In the 1970s and 1980s, Bulgaria, Czechoslovakia, and East Germany were the principal Soviet proxies for arms transfers to the Third World. These NSWP countries supplied Soviet- manufactured equipment, spare parts, and training personnel to various Third World armies. During this period, the Soviet Union also relied on its East European allies to provide the bulk of the economic aid and credits given by the Soviet Union and Eastern Europe to the countries of the Third World." Library of Congress, FRD, country studies: http://lcweb2.loc.gov/frd/cs/soviet_union/su_appn.html [accessed October 14, 2011]. That's why economies of Soviet bloc after the series of revolutions suffered such a deep shock. The economy was literally based on illegal arms trade.

[xxxi] "The effort to pull power and ownership back to the state to be "properly" redistributed revealed the underlying political battle. It was not the battle between Light and Darkness presented to western on-lookers; it was the conflict between two very different strategies out of communism. The battle was between: (1) the new "dean" post-socialist revolutionaries - those who emerged from internal or external exile, relatively untainted by the old system, armed with free-market rhetoric, and well-connected to western aid sources - to take over after the democratic revolutions of '89-90, and (2) the old "embedded" decentralizing reformers--those who worked against the old system from within and who generally had social democratic views but were dismissed as "nomenklatura" by the new "dean" revolutionaries. In a nutshell, "voucher privatization" was essentially the cover-story for the power plays of the new "dean" post-socialist revolutionaries against the old "embedded" decentralizing reformers. (Ellerman: Lessons from voucher privatization)

Old communist and StB cadres and networks, as the only people with demonstrable expertise and experience, migrated into newly established, democratic structures, and supposedly completely changed their way of thinking in order to fit in the new democratic, regime. This practice was in conflict with the requirement of so-called Civic Commissions, which were meant to ensure that this personal continuity with communist state administration is broken. This statement is not in conflict with Ellerman's analysis, as the pool of new cadres for transformation was strictly kept within established old cadres' families.

2.4.2 Security apparatus (Old cheese in new packaging)

To everyone's astonishment, the recently published EZO database[118] contained roughly 900.000 (!) names of persons in whom the StB was interested, including 200.000 persons who migrated from the category of StB cadres into the new security structures. This was the reason why this database could not be published, according to the director of the Institute for Study of Totalitarian Regimes Mgr Daniel Herman. This continuity of cadres with their sense of impunity for abuse of power can prove to be a significant challenge.

One of the witnesses of transfer of communist cadres into new security apparatus, Pavel Trhlík, was found beaten to death in the building of Meopta, Přerov. Pavel Trhlík was one of the sources of Cpt. Vladimír Hučín[119] from times when he was still working in BIS on left extremism and subversion of the state administration. One of the charges against Hučín was disobedience of an order to disclose his sources to his superiors after several very ugly deaths.

Considering the total population headcount and the numbers of members of the Communist Party, Peoples' Militia, Revolutionary Trade Union, Association of Czech-Soviet Friendship, StB informers registered in the Cibulka's list[120] (which was in fact obtained by David Eleder[121], who together with his brother accidentally drowned while on holiday at lake Bled in Croatia), one wonders how many people were in fact involved in any type of resistance against the regime. Vaclav Havel[122] in his speech to the anniversary of death of David Eleder complained that now the entire nation will judge their neighbors based on presence in the Cibulka's list. Most people opted for amnesia and dead silence.

As pointed out in the paper "Overcoming the legacies of dictatorship" by Tina Rosenberg[123], the regimes in Eastern Europe were spreading its tentacles wide across the whole population of the state. But when the regime finally crumbled, majority of the population welcomed the change, and was more than happy to start living by new, more transparent rules.

As far as I can see it, there is a danger of exclusion of large numbers of people from public service based on their past or present political beliefs, what can result exactly in the same situation as after the WW1. At the same time, documented abuse of power and crimes against humanity should be followed up and prosecuted no matter how much time from the crime passed.

Another concern is the fact that the very nature of StB work was to collect as much compromising material on everyone who could possibly become a player in public life. Operation Asanace (Sanitation) led to forced emigration of dissidents and political activists who were not responsive to pressure, blackmail, and incentives. Operation Norbert (to round up the most dangerous "elements" and dispose of them physically before the revolution) was planned but not performed. This opens serious question how real is the danger of a puppet government in a country where large proportion of the population has a file with compromising material in God-knows-whose hands. The only good news is that materials from pre-revolutionary era are slowly becoming obsolete. In addition, in Czech lands, people got so numb to scandals that in a case of a politician, hardly anything is considered an ethical problem. When Andrej Babiš's file circulated in the Parliament, several people got really scared. All others barely raised eyes from their beer glass. Vaclav Klaus's adventures as described by Eringer[124] then became part of folklore.

2.4.3 Defense

Havel's position in early 1990's was very difficult. Not only he inherited state administration loyal to a different power, economy which had to be rebuilt to the core because it was effectively based on arms trade with embargoed countries[XXXII]; but also population which suffered several waves of emigration and 60 years of systematic destruction of the

---

XXXII "Soviet watchers can point to a host of evidence indicating that the so-called collapse was engineered to disarm the West and garner billions in direct aid to Russia while inducing the West to take over the economic burden of the former satellite states that Russia could no longer support." Joel Skousen: Cancelled US missile shield signals new race to war. September 25, 2009.

best people the nation produced. One of the first announcements in Havel's career was acknowledgement of 1000 tons of Semtex sold by Czechoslovakia to Libyan dictator Muammar Kaddafi[125].

In July 1991, Havel signed the instruments of ratification of the treaty on conventional forces in Europe [CFE], a document which was signed in November 1990. Implementation of the treaty did considerably decrease the concentration of conventional armed forces in Europe. In July 1991, Czech Army had to publicly face the fact that there were 24 SS-23[XXXIII] Soviet made missiles on its territory, but denied any knowledge of nuclear warheads[126]. In fact, these SS-23 missiles were sneakily deployed in Eastern Europe by the Soviet Union in 1986, before signing the INF treaty from December 8, 1987 on liquidation of all nuclear missiles in Europe including SS-23s. Instead, Soviet Union secretly rushed the SS-23s to East Germany, Czechoslovakia and Bulgaria right before signing the treaty, and never declared them or destroyed them[127].

Czech political representation had a unique opportunity to step out of the shadow of increasingly authoritarian Russia, when the USA came up with a proposal to place a tracking radar on its territory as a part of the anti-missile shield. Czechs messed around for several years[128] and eventually chickened out and refused to participate[129]. This failure to participate in common defense shifted the country back in Russian sphere of influence more than any other single act post 1989. The anti-missile defense was eventually implemented on September 15, 2011, in Romania and Poland (interceptors), and Turkey (radar)[130].

In 2003, Vladimír Špidla's cabinet approved Czech national security strategy[131], which aligned the interests of the Czech Republic fully with

---

[XXXIII] "The USSR has carried out in full its obligations in accordance with the treaty on medium- and shorter-range missiles and with regard to "SS-23" missiles. This was stated at a briefing in the USSR Foreign Ministry press center by Vitaliy Churkin, chief of the Information Department of the USSR Foreign Ministry in connection with the fact that an attempt has again been made recently to raise the issue of the "SS-23" missiles belonging to Bulgaria, Czechoslovakia, and Germany in the context of the observance of the treaty on medium- and shorter-range missiles by the USSR. As far as the aforementioned missiles are concerned— those deployed by the Soviet Union in the GDR, Bulgaria, and Czechoslovakia during 1985 and 1986—he noted that these are the property of the above-named countries, that they are on their territories, and that they do not fall within the jurisdiction of the treaty on medium- and shorter-range missiles." (July 24, 1991; JPRS Report). In short: yes, they were there. How embarrassing for Czech military counter-intelligence.

NATO, EU, UN, and OSCE. Strong transatlantic link is also emphasized in the Military strategy from 2008[132]. The long awaited new National Security Strategy was finally approved in September 2011[133]. Its text in paragraph (32) says:

"Active involvement in the NATO system of collective defense based on a strong transatlantic link is vital to the defense of the Czech Republic. The Czech Republic supports measures designed to strengthen Article 5 of the Washington Treaty[XXXIV], and contributes to the development of the Alliance's capabilities and assets and to NATO's adaptation to the new security environment."

I personally think that over-reliance on Article 5 and reluctance to participate in common defense is highly likely to result in "dirt bag" situation as known from Special Forces training[134]. This concept is difficult to explain to a country where Special Forces engage in entirely different type of activities, namely abduction of family members of journalists who dare to participate in research on medical experiments on U.S. POWs conducted by Czech scientists during the communist era[XXXV]. The mindset is not quite the same.

2.4.4 Back to Square 1?

This overview of 20 years of development may look a little bit too brief. The events I chose are only those I consider crucial for democratic development in the Czech Republic. Just like before the WW2, and later

---

[XXXIV] "The Parties agree that an armed attack against one or more of them in Europe or North America shall be considered an attack against them all and consequently they agree that, if such an armed attack occurs, each of them, in exercise of the right of individual or collective self-defence recognised by Article 51 of the Charter of the United Nations, will assist the Party or Parties so attacked by taking forthwith, individually and in concert with the other Parties, such action as it deems necessary, including the use of armed force, to restore and maintain the security of the North Atlantic area. Any such armed attack and all measures taken as a result thereof shall immediately be reported to the Security Council. Such measures shall be terminated when the Security Council has taken the measures necessary to restore and maintain international peace and security." Available at http://www.nato.int/terrorism/five.htm [accessed October 15, 2011]

[XXXV] Angelo Catalano, then 21, was abducted by a group of Czech SF soldiers and cut by a knife on his neck. Hana Catalano, among other works, participated in documentary Mengeles Erben. Rogue Czech SF soldiers go to jail. http://www.anticomm.co.uk/?p=2522 [accessed October 15, 2011]

before the communist putsch, the Czech Republic is trying to make no commitments, and look both ways. It did not work in the past, and it is not going to work now, either. Freedom is paid by blood and outsourcing defense to allies does not work.

References

[72] August F, Beneš J: Ve znamení temna: sovětská špionážní a podvratná činnost proti Československu v letech 1918-1969; pages 34-48. Votobia, 2001 (original: Indiana University)

[73] Moravec F: Špión jemuž neveřili. Academia 2002.

[74] Česká Národní Rada: Armáda a národ. Nakladatelství Mazáč 1938.

[75] Declaration of war between Czechoslovakia and states which are at war with Great Britain, USSR, and the USA; signed on December 16, 1941 in London by Dr. Šrámek and Dr. Edvard Beneš. Reprinted in: R. Kvaček, J. Kuklík, H. Mandelová, I. Pařízková: "XX. Století o sobě. Dějiny v dokumentech;" Dialog 2005.

[76] Brown, A: Airmen in exile. Sutton Publishing, 2000.

[77] August F, Beneš J: Ve znamení temna: sovětská špionážní a podvratná činnost proti Československu v letech 1918-1969; Votobia, 2001 (original: Indiana University) – That was telegram from May 24, 1918. (page 22). This order caused quite a lot of havoc at that time. R. Kvaček, J. Kuklík, H. Mandelová, I. Pařízková: "XX. Století o sobě. Dějiny v dokumentech;" Dialog 2005; in chapter about the Beneš's meeting with Stalin in Moscow (11-12 Dec 1943) claim that Beneš met Stalin once before, in 1935 (Treaty of Czechoslovak-Soviet friendship)

[78] August F, Beneš J: Ve znamení temna: sovětská špionážní a podvratná činnost proti Československu v letech 1918-1969; Votobia, 2001 (original: Indiana University). Page 31. Hašek was sent by kominterna back to Czechoslovakia (to Kladno), but never picked up on his assignments. He died shortly after he started writing his memoirs from Russia.

[79] Beneš J: Čas voněl snem. Primus 2005. Edvard Beneš made reports about the real situation in Bolshevik Russia confidential. They were declassified only after 1938 (Protectorate), when the public refused to believe it. This is in striking contrast with M.R. Štefánik, who got Bolshevik agitators in Russia under arrest.

[80] Handwritten notes of President Truman Notes by Harry S. Truman on the Potsdam Conference, July 16, 1945. President's Secretary's File, Truman Papers. Harry S. Truman Library and Museum.
http://www.trumanlibrary.org/whistlestop/study_collections/bomb/large/documen ts/index.php?pagenumber=2&documentid=1&documentdate=1945-07-16&studycollectionid=abomb&groupid= [accessed October 14, 2011]

[81] FCAFA: Victims of Communism
http://fcafa.wordpress.com/2010/08/15/victims-of-communism-3/ [accessed October 14, 2011]

[82] Oxford Dictionary of National Biography: Karel Janousek
http://www.oxforddnb.com/index/93/101093047/ [accessed October 14, 2011]; More information in Czech is available at Protikomunistické Místo: http://protikomunisticke.misto.cz/svedectvi/5e.htm [accessed October 14, 2011]

[83] Jaroslav Pospisil: Hyeny, Lípa Vizovice 2002; http://knihy.abz.cz/prodej/hyeny [accessed October 14, 2011]; Hyeny v akci, Lípa, Vizovice 2003. http://knihy.abz.cz/prodej/hyeny-v-akci [accessed October 14, 2011]. This book presents transfer of Nazi criminals in Communist structures; and communist terror and anticommunist resistance in South Moravia, mainly the Zlín region.

[84] Resistance group Svetlana – documents from the Museum of Third Resistance, Příbram. Available at http://www.anticomm.co.uk/?p=1097 [accessed October 14, 2011]; Šedivý ZF: Světlana. Published by Ing Ladislav Štěrba – Papyrus; Lišková M: Organizace Světlana. Studie o působení protikomunistické odbojové skupiny na Zlínsku v letech 1948 – 1952; Brno 2011. Online available at: http://is.muni.cz/th/341711/ff_b/Bakalarska_diplomova_prace.doc [October 14, 2011]

[85] Lukeš I: A Cold War Dangle Operation with an American Dimension. Operation Kámen. Ensnaring the Unwitting in Czechoslovakia. Studies in Intelligence – Journal of the American Intelligence Professional. Unclassified articles from Studies in Intelligence Volume 55, Number 1, (March 2011). https://www.cia.gov/library/center-for-the-study-of-intelligence/csi-publications/csi-studies/studies/vol.-55-no.-1/kamen-a-cold-war-dangle-operation-with-an-american-dimension-1948-1952.html [accessed October 14, 2011]

[86] Bursík T: Osud odbojové organizace Černý Lev 777. Published by OABS MV, Czech Republic, 2007.

[87] Masin B: Gauntlet. Naval Institute Press; 2006.

[88] Politbureau: Silver Fox resistance group. On the Re-Examination of the Criminal Case against Petr Křivka and Co. December 1957. http://www.anticomm.co.uk/?p=241 [accessed October 14, 2011]

[89] Stehlík E: Příspěvek k historii Czechoslovak Intelligence Organization - CIO (1948-1957). Obtained from the Museum of Third Resistance. http://www.anticomm.co.uk/wp-content/uploads/2011/05/TAB3h1.jpg [accessed October 14, 2011]

[90] Yalta Conference in the Crimea between the Soviet Union, UK and US, 1945. Documents available at the National Archives Kew Garden: http://yourarchives.nationalarchives.gov.uk/index.php?title=Yalta_Conference_in_t he_Crimea_between_the_Soviet_Union%2C_UK_and_US%2C_1945 [accessed June 4, 2011]

[91] Several tons of archiving material and research and other works available in the Institute for study of totalitarian regimes (USTR), Security Services Archive (SSA), Bureau for Documentation and Investigation of Communist Crimes (UDV), Institute for Contemporary History (ICH).

[92] Schovánek Radek: Organizační vývoj technických složek MV 1948-1989 in Securitas Imperii 1 a 2, ÚDV 1994.

[93] Lockwood Jonathan Samuel, Lockwood Kathleen O'Brien: Russian view of US strategy, Its Past, its future. Transaction Publishers, 1993.

[94] Suvorov Viktor: Inside the aquarium - Making a top Soviet spy. MacMillan 1985.

[95] Moore David T: Critical thinking and intelligence analysis. National Defense Intelligence College, Mar 2007. http://www.ndic.edu/press/2641.htm [accessed October 14, 2011]

[96] Andrew C, Gordievsky O: KGB: The Inside Story of Its Foreign Operations from Lenin to Gorbachev Harpercollins; 1st edition (May 1992)

[97] Andrew C, Gordievsky O: More Instructions from the Centre: Top Secret Files on KGB Global Operations 1975-1985. Routledge; 1 edition (April 30, 1992)

[98] Andrew C, Gordievsky O: Comrade Kryuchkov's Instructions: Top Secret Files on KGB Foreign Operations, 1975-1985. Stanford University Press (February 1, 1994)

[99] Andrew C, Mitrokhin V: The Mitrokhin Archive The Sword and the Shield: The Mitrokhin Archive and the Secret History of the KGB. Basic Books (September 5, 2000).

[100] Barron J: Mig Pilot: The Final Escape of Lieutenant Belenko. Mcgraw-Hill; First Edition edition (February 1980)

[101] Czechoslovakia in 1968. That was than 1968; available at http://thatwasthen1968.com/news/czech1.htm [accessed October 14, 2011, 2011]

[102] Daniliauskas, J: How significant was Alexander Dubcek in the development of reformist communism? The University of Hull, Department of politics. The politics of Eastern Europe; 1995. Available at http://works.tarefer.ru/32/100223/index.html [accessed October 14, 2011]

[103] Talks between Dubcek and Breznev in Cierna nad Tisou (July 29, 1968) and Bratislava (Aug 3, 1968). Soviet side demanded the Czechs to get rid of Josef Smrkovský, and František Kriegel, and dissolution of civic organizations KAN and K231. Talks at Cross-purposes. Available at www.praha.eu [accessed June 4, 2011]

[104] CPSU CC Politburo Message to Alexander Dubček, August 13, 1968. http://library.thinkquest.org/C001155/documents/doc46.htm [accessed June 4, 2011]

[105] Document No. 81: Transcript of Leonid Brezhnev's Telephone Conversation with Alexander Dubček, August 13, 1968. The Prague Spring Foundation. Available at http://www.gwu.edu/~nsarchiv/nsa/publications/DOC_readers/psread/doc81.htm [accessed June 4, 2011]

[106] Invitation letter: the letter was written by Antonín Kapek and signed by Vasil Bilak, Alois Indra, Antonín Kapek, Drahomír Kolder, and Oldřich Švestka. http://www.praha.eu/jnp/en/extra/Year_68/august/short_story_of_the_invitation_letter.html [accessed October 14, 2011, 2011]

[107] Institute for study of totalitarian regimes: newly published documents obtained from Ukraine on invasion 1968 http://www.ustrcr.cz/cs/dokumenty-kgb [accessed October 14, 2011]

[108] Frolík J: Špión vypovídá. Orbis 1990.

[109] Vachalovský P, Bok J: Špión vypovídá II. J. W. Hill, 2000. Original from the University of Michigan.

[110] Sejna J: We will bury you. Sidgwick & Jackson (August 1985)

[111] Douglass J: Red Cocaine: The drugging of America. Second Opinion Pub Inc, First Edition (1990)

[112] Monographs of the Bureau for Documentations and Investigation of Communist Crimes. http://aplikace.mvcr.cz/archiv2008/policie/udv/securita/#1 [accessed October 14, 2011]; http://aplikace.mvcr.cz/archiv2008/policie/udv/sesity/ [accessed October 14, 2011]

[113] Mengeles Erben, Documentary of Arte TV. Available at http://www.youtube.com/watch?v=dfN3QQnDLjI [accessed October 14, 2011]

[114] Douglass J: Betrayed. 1st Book Library (June 14, 2002).

[115] Kremen P: Nikomu jsem neublizil (I harmed no one) – documentary about an StB agent, which reflects the way of thinking of people who often dumped their closest friends and relatives for meagre reward or promise of impunity in various usually low-level offenses. http://www.ceskatelevize.cz/porady/10267494987-nikomu-jsem-neublizil/21056226956/ [accessed October 14, 2011]

[116] Ellerman D: Lessons From East Europe's Voucher Privatization. http://cog.kent.edu/lib/Ellerman5.htm [accessed October 14, 2011]

[117] Kraske M, Puhl J: Eastern Europe's economic boom: The tiny tigers. Der Spiegel, December 2005. http://www.spiegel.de/international/spiegel/0,1518,391649,00.html [accessed October 14, 2011]

[118] Record of the Senate discussion on USTR: http://www.anticomm.co.uk/?p=353 [accessed October 14, 2011]

[119] Catalanová H: Bolshevik Inquisition (The case of Vladimír Hučín) http://www.jrnyquist.com/bolshevik_inquisition_1.htm [accessed 30 May 2011]

[120] The list of StB confidents obtained by Petr Cibulka and David Eleder, http://www.cibulka.com [accessed October 14, 2011]

[121] Vanek J: Věnováno desátému výročí tragické smrti Davida Eledera (Dedicated to the 10th anniversary of death of David Eleder. http://www.virtually.cz/starydesign/2202/vanek.html [accessed October 14, 2011]

[122] Havel V: Samozvaní samosoudci, jeden z největších úspěchů StB. Britské Listy. Speech from December 1993. http://blisty.cz/art/32645.html [accessed October 14, 2011]

[123] Rosenberg T: Overcoming the legacies of dictatorship. http://www.foreignaffairs.com/articles/50981/tina-rosenberg/overcoming-the-legacies-of-dictatorship [accessed October 14, 2011]

[124] Eringer R: Vadav Klaus exposed. The Investigator, Santa Barbara News Press, December 20th, 2008. http://recolumns.blogspot.com/2010/10/vadac-klaus-exposed.html [accessed October 14, 2011]

[125] Frankel G: Havel details sale of explosives to Libya. Washington Post, March 23, 1990. http://www.washingtonpost.com/wp-srv/inatl/longterm/panam103/stories/libya0390.htm [accessed October 14, 2011]

[126] JPRS Report: JPRS-TAC-91-019; August 8, 1991; Arms Control. Available at: http://www.dtic.mil/cgi-bin/GetTRDoc?Location=U2&doc=GetTRDoc.pdf&AD=ADA345466 [accessed October 14, 2011]

[127] Skousen J: Cancelled US missile shield signals new race to war. World Affairs brief, Rense.com. September 25, 2009. http://www.rense.com/general87/cancel.htm [accessed October 14, 2011]

[128] Hildreth SA, Ek C: Long-range ballistic missile defense in Europe. Congressional Research Service, 2009. http://www.fas.org/sgp/crs/weapons/RL34051.pdf [accessed October 15, 2011]

[129] Czech Republic exits U.S. missile shield plans. Defense News, June 15, 2011. http://www.defensenews.com/story.php?i=6824203 [accessed October 15, 2011]

[130] Implementing missile defense in Europe. September 15, 2011; DTIRP. http://dtirp.dtra.mil/NC/displayArticle.aspx?displayFile=G/g_15sep11.htm [accessed October 15, 2011]

[131] Narodní Bezpečnostní Strategie České Republiky, 2003; Czech version: http://www.vlada.cz/assets/ppov/brs/dokumenty/bezpecnostni_strategie_2003.pdf [accessed October 15, 2011]; and English (web of Czech Ministry of Foreign Affairs in Berlin): http://www.mzv.cz/berlin/de/informationen_uber_tschechien/politik/aussenpolitik/sicherheitsstrategie_der_tschechischen/index.html [accessed October 15, 2011]

[132] The Military strategy of the Czech Republic. Prague 2008. http://merln.ndu.edu/whitepapers/Czech_Republic_English-2008.pdf [accessed October 15, 2011]

[133] National Security Strategy of the Czech Republic, September 2011. http://www.mocr.army.cz/images/id_8001_9000/8503/Czech_Security_Strategy_2011.pdf [accessed October 15, 2011]

[134] Ranger handbook. Not for the weak, not for the faint-hearted. U.S. Army SH 21-76; Ranger training brigade, United States Army Infantry School, Fort Benning, Georgia. July 2006.

3   ELECTORAL SYSTEM

3.1   Suffrage in Czechoslovakia

Suffrage in the founding documents was defined as universal, for all citizens both male and female, first from 26, later changed to 18 years of age. During the period under German Protectorate, these provisions became obsolete. During the first post-war elections in 1946, large groups of the population were excluded from elections based on nationality, and many Slavic nationals, namely coming Soviet army, were allowed to participate in elections although they were not Czechoslovak citizens.

The situation after the coup 1948 made voting compulsory, whilst removing the factor of choice, what created the hilarious effect of 99% popular support for elected officials, and gave the regime powerful argument that the communist rule over the country is indeed consensual. At the same time, convicted criminals were stripped of their "honorary citizenship rights" as part of their sentence[135], what excluded large parts of population from the electorate. Today, many of these convicted criminals are considered political prisoners, and their sentences were rehabilitated[136]. Nevertheless, in real time, their exclusion from the electorate, both active and passive, helped the regime to maintain its grip over the subjugated population.

It is worth mentioning the case of Pavel Wonka and his attempt to run for a public office. Wonka was imprisoned, denied medical care, and died at age 35 only a few days after being sentenced to another term in prison. Judge Marcela Horváthová, who insisted on imprisonment despite being aware of Wonka's poor health[137], is still in public service. Ethical concerns over this sentence were repeatedly discussed, but did not re sult in serious legal action.

After 1989, the right to vote became easier to exercise without the fear of punishment. It is no longer compulsory to participate in elections; and the factor of choice reappeared. There are some concerns that some people have a problem to participate in elections because of troubles with permanent residence and inability to register as voters, and even occasional reports of people who appear "erased" from the database of inhabitants. Silent exclusion of expatriates and especially young people who live outside their permanent residence or abroad is one of taboos of Czech electoral system, which considerably distorts the results.

3.2   Electoral system and institutions

The Constitution 1992 re-introduced multiparty democracy, with proportional representation in two chambers of Parliament; and a combination of district, winner take all, and proportional representation hybrid system. In theory the system is robust and difficult to abuse by any particular party. As concluded by Shapiro in his essay "The meaning of American democracy", where he analyzed institutional and procedural democracy, substantive democracy, and briefly described historical development; the fact that different states use different method of voting does not mean the system is not democratic. In optimal situation, democracy as a system of government develops towards a regime which is "both free and stable" towards polyarchal democracy. As I can see it, the real issues in Czech Republic are not in the electoral system or institutions, but its substantive part, meaning how the ideas described on paper are implemented in practice[138].

3.3   Voting power

Political advertising clearly gives advantage to those who have the resources to pay for extensive billboard campaigns, without asking too many questions where the money comes from – or if so, way too late, because the deal is already done. Total number of advertising spaces is difficult to control. Financing of electoral campaigns has been a problem since the first elections after 1989.

Another substantial problem has its origin in the nature of StB work and the fact that this service excelled in collecting of compromising material on anyone who had the potential to become important in any way. As the material from the communist era ages, it is slowly becoming less relevant and dangerous. However, as explained in detail in the report[139] of the Antoni Macierewicz Commission in Poland, the continuity of personnel, procedures, and methods of work, and to a certain extent also networks and mindset; this principle of control of political and economic life through compromising material systematically collected by current security services is still widely used. This practice is a threat to the very foundations of young democracy, because it has the potential to turn the Constitution into a formal document only, without its substantive meaning.

References:

[135] Act 231/1948 – Act on Protection of People's Democratic Republic; §52. Original text in Czech http://aplikace.mvcr.cz/archiv2008/sbirka/1948/sb85-48.pdf; English translation available at: http://www.anticomm.co.uk/?p=348 [Accessed on October 14, 2011]

[136] Zákon 198/1993 o protiprávnosti komunistického režimu (Act on unlawfulness of the communist regime). Available at http://www.sds.cz/docs/prectete/ezakon/198_1993.htm [accessed October 14, 2011]

[137] Circumstances surrounding Pavel Wonka's death reexamined. Foreign Broadcast Information Service: JPRS Report; Aug 1990. http://dodreports.com/pdf/ada372752.pdf [accessed October 14, 2011]

[138] Čestmír Hofhanzl: Roots of corruption of Czech post-communist democrature. Čestmír Hofhanzl in his articles comments on complete loss of any sense of ethics on Czech political scene, and its root cause. http://www.konzervativnistrana.cz/nazory/nase-nazory/nazor/article/koreny-korupce-ceske-postkomunisticke-demokratury.html [accessed October 14, 2011]

[139] The President of Verification Commission Antoni Macierewicz: Macierewicz Report on liquidation of the Polish Military Information Services ridden with KGB agents. http://www.archive.org/details/MacierewiczReportOnLiquidationOfThePolishMilitaryInformationServices [accessed October 14, 2011]

4 THE POWER OF MEDIA

Access to alternative sources of information is one of the key conditions for functional democracy, and it is closely connected to the freedom of expression. The idea is based on the logic that people with free access to different sources of information will choose whatever they wish to listen to, and eventually the majority will reject or dismiss extremes. Inclusion of minority views and their free confrontation is eventually likely to merge with mainstream, in the difference from isolated groups in non-free societies where information blockade creates the effect of distorted reality as perceived by a fish in a bowl[140].

Although censorship was formally abolished[141], some people would like to have it back[142, 143] to a certain degree – especially when sexual affairs of celebrities get into too much detail as in the case of Monica Lewinski; when witch-hunt in the media results in the target's death as in the case of Rachel Jackson, wife of President Andrew Jackson[144, 145], or when sensitive documents get leaked[146, 147].

Media have a great power to spread misinformation[148], and restrict access to important news by selection bias[XXXVI], and failure to differentiate between hard news (information) and political commentary (interpretation of the event, opinion). Timing of affairs indicates systematic exploitation of all sorts of secret information sources, including illegal wiretapping by thousands of registered security agencies.

In the Czech Republic, the biggest problem as I can see it is the language limitation what makes minority press and other media economically non-viable. But some serious well prepared magazines are still able to survive on the market, what means that the public is not completely apathetic. Internet changed information flow substantially, and opened access to non-Czech sources free of charge. How many people are using the internet for learning and serious reading is a different question.

[XXXVI] Major security issues such as important agreements and their impact are often not part of mainstream news, and the general public is totally unaware of them. One of the examples is deployment of Russian P-800 Yakhont missiles to Syria, which was completely blanked by the mainstream media.
http://www.ynetnews.com/articles/0,7340,L-3955585,00.html [accessed October 15, 2011]

Another major issue is the quality of Czech television broadcasting[149], and the vulnerability of Czech broadcasting council to political pressures. Brief look at the program of Czech TV after a period spent abroad works like a time machine back to the normalization era. The movies are the same, the shows are the same, and even the faces changed only with respect to their age. Scary is that this communist theme park is taken seriously as the most important source of news by vast majority of the population.

References

[140] Hawking S, Mlodinow L: Stephen Hawking Asks, What Is Reality? Time Magazine.   http://www.time.com/time/arts/article/0,8599,2017262,00.html [accessed October 15, 2011]

[141] CEFRES institute Workshop Film mezi kontrolou a službou moci (Film between control and servility to power http://www.cefs.cz/dokumenty/cefres.pdf [accessed October 15, 2011]

[142]   Serious   discussion   on   the   extent   of   censorship: http://www.serendipity.li/cda.html [accessed October 15, 2011]

[143]   Google   censorship   tools: http://www.bbc.co.uk/news/technology-11380677 [accessed October 15, 2011]

[144] The case of Andrew Jackson's wife Rachel who died of heart attack caused by stress related to the witch-hunt in pro-Adams newspapers. Available at History Net: http://www.historynet.com/andrew-jackson-the-petticoat-affair-scandal-in-jackons-white-house.htm/2. [accessed October 15, 2011]

[145] NNDB: Rachel Jackson, born Jun 1767, died 22 Dec 1828. Biography as published at NNDB. http://www.nndb.com/people/855/000126477/ [accessed October 15, 2011]

[146] US State Department: Remarks to the Press on Release of Purportedly Confidential   Documents   by   Wikileaks   (November   29,   2010). http://www.state.gov/secretary/rm/2010/11/152078.htm [accessed October 15, 2011]

[147] Doyle C: Extraterritorial application of US Criminal Law. Congressional Research Service, March 2010. http://www.fas.org/sgp/crs/misc/94-166.pdf [accessed Octoer 15, 2011]

[148] Kull S, Ramsay C, Lewis E: Misperceptions, the Media, and the Iraq War. The Meaning of American democracy. Political Science Quarterly, Summer 2005.

[149] International Press Institute: Global network for a free media. Press Freedom audit   report   –   Czech   Republic.   IPI   Mission   May   2009   . http://www.ifex.org/czech_republic/2009/10/15/press_freedom_audit_report_cze ch_republic.pdf [accessed October 15, 2011]

5 CONDITIONS OF POLYARCHAL DEMOCRACY

The line between democratic and authoritarian regime is blurred. Virtually all totalitarian regimes call themselves democratic, claiming that organizing elections at more or less regular intervals is enough.

5.1   Elected representation Currently, there is a debate in the Senate whether the President should be elected directly by the public. In my opinion, it does not matter that much whether the president is elected one way or the other; what matters is selection of candidates who run for the office. What is a disaster are people who are directly and openly controlled by foreign (Soviet and later Russian) intelligence service and the public thinks it's perfectly fine (see Eringer's article about Klaus). It is necessary to pay attention to the selection of candidates for a public office, to make sure the support comes from a safe source. Origin of money traceable to former Soviet Union and their security services should be considered a major security threat, much more than mere presence on some of the above mentioned lists. This threat is also described in detail in the Macierewicz report.

Foreign security services prefer public servants who can be "handled" or "controlled". No binding act necessary; the point is that the person is responsive to pressure, threats, and incentives facilitated by compromising material[150], and exploitation of greed and desire for power. These methods are consistent with the findings from the Macierewicz report. Czech counter-intelligence service is scared to death of politically active independent citizens, even those who are no longer Czech citizens living abroad.

Efforts to infiltrate every civic organization, to make sure they are kept under control, is in direct violation of another arch of functional democracy – right to assemble and form independent associations. The practice is in detail explained in the Macierewicz report, but in fact it is considered common knowledge. The most graphic example of this practice in Czech conditions is situation within the Confederation of Political Prisoners.

5.2   Free, fair, and frequent elections

Elections in the Czech Republic are always a great topic to follow. It would be nice to know how many people have problem to register as voters due to issues with their permanent residence, and how many people are excluded because they live abroad. Another area of concern is harassment of candidates for public office, and their intimidation. Surprisingly, electoral process is not considered a problem as per Jeremy Druker's report "Nations in transit ratings and average scores"[151].

5.3   Alternative sources of information

Sadly, most Czechs still do not speak or read other languages than Czech (or Slovak) well enough to be able to comfortably access other sources of information, including international news. This language insufficiency might in fact be encouraged by the elites through no will to enforce standards in language education. Prepaid TV in English is still not expense most families tolerate; the same applies to foreign newspapers and books.

Intimidation of journalists and outspoken citizens is not conducted through physical violence, but through threats of redundancy and cessation of contracts. Suspicious deaths of independent journalists and historians occasionally occur, but are difficult to prove due to limited access to medical files, and confounding factors. Slovak dissident, Minister of Interior in early 1990's, and later director of the Institute for National Memory Jan Langoš[152, 153, 154] died in a car accident in June 2006. As per the Reporters without borders, in 2009, Czech journalist Sabina Slonková was convicted for failure to disclose her sources of information to the court[155].

This combination of denied access to information, selection bias by the media, and difficulty to access alternative sources of information creates distorted perception of reality, which is extremely difficult to understand from outside. Main source of alternative information is internet, with its hundreds and thousands of various blogs; most important of them written by expats. Sadly, there are growing concerns about the censorship of internet, and even blocking Google search engine completely (Prague 4 free internet service provided by the Ministry of Interior). Those, who really do need internet regularly, switch to a paid service, whilst occasional users or pensioners are likely happy to get on with the Seznam.cz catalogue in Czech.

International news channels are still very difficult to access through cable TV. This virtual monopoly over major information flows creates conditions ideal for manipulation with public opinion, as there is relatively limited access to alternative information sources. The only English speaking radio I was able to get in Opava in 2004-2006 was official broadcasting of Radio China which had some station nearby. Czech Republic is a small market and high quality books are scarce. Some highly important and controversial books such as e.g. Jan Beneš: Čas voněl snem[156] (alternative history of communist party of USSR) were dumped after publishing and majority of published copies never made it to bookstores. In environment like this, a key condition of functional democracy, consent of the people with the ruling elite based on enlightened understanding, is very difficult to achieve.

5.4   Freedom of expression

People who are used to live in "internal exile" prefer not to engage in politics unless forced by circumstances to do so. In addition, this tactics of avoidance is considered normal and healthy by majority. Those who are outspoken and get beaten by the system are then condemned by the general public, as fools who failed to respect the rules of engagement. Decades of fear-conditioning caused all pervasive fear and reluctance of the population to express minority opinion. Logical consequence of this situation, escape to banal chatter, makes enlightened understanding of outside reality which is crucial for functional democracy extremely limited.

Historical legacy and general reluctance to deal with ghosts from the past (even implemented in the legal system, like e.g. the Meritorious President Beneš Act[157]); reluctance to replace long serving teachers of history and social sciences; avoidance of confrontation of unpleasant historical facts and hiding behind official unchallenged version, no matter how untrue it is, bring nostalgic moods and idealized memories of the past.

Mindset of civil servants and the population in general is to treat its own citizens and dependants as a potential threat which has to be suppressed instead of a resource which should be developed. This is consistent with the findings of Robert Buchar in his book "And reality be damned[158]". Outspoken individuals are getting punished by their own community including close family because they are clearly seen as a threat. This comes from the deep sub-consciousness of historical experience from times when punishment of whole family for one emigrant or political dissident was standard response of the regime. In essence, the state does not have to use power to suppress public disobedience, as "breaking of the back" of dependent and outspoken or independent members of the community is already done in the family or in the respective community. Person who became an "enemy of the state" represents threat to the entire family, or community, respectively. Fear conditioning works even when the threat is over. This transfer of family memory and life skills is nicely explained in the book Between Generations[159]. Silent citizens may be perfect subjects for an authoritarian ruler; they would be disaster for a democracy.

5.5   Associational autonomy

Freedom to form associations and clubs, including political parties, is guaranteed, and in theory not limited in any way. Historically, there is still significant reluctance for organized activities of any kind, because literally all such associations were infiltrated by StB informers, and this fact was general knowledge. From the Macierewicz Report on liquidation of Polish Military Information Services, chapter Surveillance of the internal social and political environment, we learn how the practice of intensive monitoring of associations by the WSI continued in virtually identical manner as before 1989. On the example of Charter 77, where more than 70% of participants were already at the time of signature or later became StB informers, how the State secret police managed to not only infiltrate, but also create associations in order to lure persons of interest and targets of surveillance.

Recent example of such situation can be found in the case of Confederation of Political Prisoners, which is now led by a person whose file from the 1950's got lost, and who spent 18 years at communist Ministry of Work and Social Affairs. In essence, potentially "dangerous" independent associations are systematically targeted and subverted in order to create as much chaos within their ranks as possible, and paralyze any substantial political activity. Independent organizations have very limited chances to become serious players on the political scene.

Control of political opposition, civic associations, and individual citizens was exercised through this ministry, which played a key role in keeping the regime in power. As per Jaroslav Spurný[160] – the only ministry which matters today is the Ministry of Interior, a fact what suggests that very little has changed since those days.

5.6   Inclusive citizenship

Mindset of leaders at all levels which promotes mediocrity instead of talents, and rewarding loyalty at the expense of merit. This creates the effect known as "sticky floor" for potential rivals and stalls careers of new generation of potential leaders, and effectively prevents creation of a new talent pool. In the situation of crisis (like the one in 1938), there is no one experienced enough who could take the lead.

In this sense, the seemingly hilarious one sentence long Lex Beneš Act explains mentality of the nation more than anything else. Beneš's achievement after the war was liquidation of disloyal economic backbone of the state, liquidation of people with combat experience ho could potentially pose a threat to him, liquidation of political opposition through creation of the National Front, and liquidation of ethnic minorities by their physical removal. This treatment of human resources is plain stupid, not even mentioning the fact of violation of numerous conventions at time of peace.

No society can withstand competition with others if it systematically disposes off its best people. This mindset, which still persists, forces people into boundaries of mediocrity, because those who stand out are certain to be screwed over. Nobody is going to back them up, because being outstanding is a crime worse than high treason.

References:

[150] Clifford T: Law school accused of mafia ties Security threat to state feared amid Plzeň university scandal Available at http://www.praguepost.com/news/2503-law-school-accused-of-mafia-ties.html [accessed June 3, 2011]

[151] Druker J: Czech Republic Nations in Transit ratings and average scores. http://www.freedomhouse.org/images/File/nit/2011/NIT-2011-Czech_Republic.pdf [accessed October 15, 2011]

[152] Lesná L: ÚPN: Ján Langoš did not lose Široký file http://spectator.sme.sk/articles/view/26423 [accessed October 15, 2011]

[153] Mastalir L: Ján Langoš, former dissident and post-1989 Czechoslovak Interior Minister, dies in an automobile accident. http://www.radio.cz/en/section/curraffrs/jan-langos-former-dissident-and-post-1989-czechoslovak-interior-ministerdies-in-an-automobile-accident [accessed October 15, 2011]

[154] Dudíková A: Ján Langoš, 59; Slovak dissident opened spy files. http://www.boston.com/news/globe/obituaries/articles/2006/06/18/jan_langos_59_slovak_dissident_opened_spy_files/ [accessed October 15, 2011]

[155] Reporters Without Borders, Journalist Sabina Slonková convicted for protecting her sources, 11 February 2009, available at: http://www.unhcr.org/refworld/docid/4993e269c.html [accessed October 15, 2011]

[156] Beneš J: Čas voněl snem. Primus 2004.

[157] Meritorious President Beneš Act 292/2004. http://iuridictum.pecina.cz/w/Lex_Bene%C5%A1 [accessed October 15, 2011]

[158] Buchar, R: And the reality be damned. Undoing America: What the media did not tell you about the end of the Cold War and the fall of communism in Europe. Strategic Publishing Group, 2009.

[159] Bertaux D, P Thompson: International Yearbook of oral history and life stories, Volume II, Between Generations: Family models, myths and memories. Oxford University Press 1993.

[160] Spurný J: Policie jako mocenský nástroj (Police as a tool of power). Respekt XXII; 16-17, 2011.

6 CONCLUSION

Functional democracy can be distorted in dysfunctional pseudo-democratic authoritative regime in many ways. The point is to look at the system from distance, identify the critical structures and tools for limiting the power, and silently remove the "right" one. People generally do not understand the system well enough to find out what's wrong until it's too late. So if the general public is focused on the "multi-party" part of the whole system, the power can be exercised by removal of a different power-limiting mechanism.

As documented by University of Hawaii "Freedom, Democide, and War" web project Power Kills[161], authoritarian regimes are the biggest cause of civilian deaths. Some democides are very obvious when they occur, but others cannot be detected until too late, especially those which do not involve mass murders.

I believe serious discussion is needed about the methods of measuring democracy in comparison to various types of totalitarian regimes; in order to develop series of methods, which would measure democratic deficit and therefore the risk and level of democide which is closely related to it more accurately.[162]

References:

[161] Rummel: Freedom, democide, war: http://www.hawaii.edu/powerkills/ [accessed October 15, 2011]

[162] IC R2P Responsibility to Protect http://www.responsibilitytoprotect.org/ http://responsibilitytoprotect.org/ICISS%20Report.pdf [accessed October 15, 2011]

APPENDIX

Czechoslovak – Soviet Treaty (Czech – Russian Agreement) signed by the Czechoslovak exile government in Moscow on December 12, 1943

Edvard Beneš's Chancellor Jaromír Smutný in his personal notes from visit of President Edvard Beneš in Moscow on December 11 to 12, 1943, described negotiations of Czech representation with Stalin. The participants representing the Czech side were Klement Gottwald, Zdenek Nejedlý, Jaromír Smutný, and Edvard Beneš. Soviet side was represented by J.V. Stalin, M.I. Kalinin, I.M. Majskij, A.M. Vasilevskij, and K.J. Vorosilov. V.M. Molotov was assisting Beneš with translations, as Beneš's Russian was not sufficient to be able to discuss the matters without an interpreter.

Source: R. Kvaček, J. Kuklík, H. Mandelová, I. Pařízková: XX. Století o sobě. Dějiny v dokumentech (XX century about itself. History in documents)

The treaty was published in the "Notice of the Ministry of Interior from January 17, 1946 on publication of the Treaty on friendship, mutual assistance, and post-war cooperation between the Czechoslovak Republic and the Union of Soviet Socialist Republics, signed in Moscow on December 12, 1943".

The treaty was signed by Z Fierlinger and V Molotov on December 12, 1943, and ratified by Edvard Beneš and Hubert Ripka on December 20, 1943. Ratification documents were exchanged in Moscow on December 22, 1943, this was confirmed by Jan Masaryk.

Treaty on friendship, mutual assistance, and post-war cooperation between Czechoslovak Republic and the USSR (translation)

President of the Czechoslovak Republic and Presidium of the Supreme Soviet of the USSR wishing to amend the existing treaty on mutual assistance existing between the Czechoslovak Republic and USSR, signed in Prague on May 16, 1935, and to confirm statements in the Agreement between the Czechoslovak Republic and the government of the USSR on common advance in the war against Germany signed on July 18, 1941 in London; wishing to cooperate after the war on maintenance of peace and prevention of another attack from the German side, and to ensure permanent friendship and post-war peaceful cooperation, decided to negotiate for this purpose an agreement and designated their assignees:

President of Czechoslovak Republic designates Zdenek Fierlinger, Ambassador of the Czechoslovak Republic in the Soviet Union, Presidium of the Supreme Soviet designates Vyacheslav Mikhailovich Molotov, Peoples' Commissar of foreign affairs, who exchanging their mandates and finding them in perfect order including its form, agreed on the following:

Article 1

High covenant parties, agreeing mutually on unification in policy of permanent friendship and friendly post-war cooperation, as well as mutual assistance, are committed to provide each other military and other assistance and support of all kinds in the current war against Germany and all states which are allied with it in offensive acts in Europe.

Article 2

High covenant parties are committed not to enter for the duration of the current war into any negotiations with Hitler's government or any other government in Germany which would not clearly surrender its offensive intentions, and which would not negotiate without mutual agreement any armistice or peace treaty with Germany or any other state allied with it in offensive acts in Europe.

Article 3

In confirmation of pre-war policy of peace and mutual assistance expressed in their agreement signed on May 16, 1935, in Prague, high covenant parties are committing themselves that in case one of the sides is dragged into war operations against Germany after the war, should it renew its policy "Drang nach Osten", or any other state which would be allied with Germany with such a war, second high covenant party immediately provides second covenant party dragged into such war operations all military and other assistance at its disposal.

Article 4

High covenant parties, bearing in mind security interests of each of them, agreed on close and friendly cooperation after re-establishment of peace, and also that they will act in line with principles of mutual respect of their independence and sovereignty, as well as non-intervention in internal affairs of a different state. They agreed to develop in terms as broad as possible their economic contacts and provide each other all possible economic aid after the war.

Article 5

Each of high covenant parties is committed not to enter any alliance or coalition directed against the other high covenant party.

Article 6

This Covenant inures immediately after signature and is subject to ratification in the shortest possible time; exchange of ratification documents will be performed in Moscow as soon as possible.

This agreement remains valid for the period of 20 years from the time of signature, whilst if one of the high covenant parties does not wish to terminate the contract toward the end of the contract expiration term by informing the other party about the intention to terminate the contract 12 months in advance, its validity extends for another 5 years, indefinitely until one of the high covenant parties doe not announce its intention to terminate the agreement 12 months in advance before the end of the 5-year period.

To confirm this, the assignees signed this agreement and added their seals. Created in two copies, one in Czechoslovak language and one in Russian. Both versions have the same validity. In Moscow, on December 12, 1943.

On behalf of the President of the Czechoslovak Republic	On behalf of the Supreme Soviet of the USSR
Zdenek Fierlinger	**V Molotov**

Protocol

At negotiation of the Treaty on friendship, mutual assistance, and post-war cooperation between the Czechoslovak republic and the USSR the high Covenant parties stated that in case any country neighboring with the Czechoslovak republic or the USSR and was subject to German attack in this war, would wish to join this treaty, this would be allowed following agreement between the governments of the Czechoslovak republic and the USSR, and in such a case the agreement would become a tri-party agreement.

On behalf of the President of the Czechoslovak Republic	*On behalf of the Supreme Soviet of the USSR*
Zdenek Fierlinger	*V Molotov*

Agreement concerning the relationship between the Czechoslovak government and the Soviet Commander in Chief on the entry of Soviet troops into Czechoslovak territory.

The treaty was signed by Minister of Foreign Affairs and a State Minister **Hubert Ripka**, who was entitled to act on behalf of the Czechoslovak exile government, with Ambassador extraordinary and plenipotentiary of the USSR to the government of the Czechoslovak Republic **V Lebedev** on May 8, 1944, in London.

This treaty effectively placed Czechoslovakia in the Soviet zone a month before the Normandy landings. In this context, it is difficult to see why Czechoslovak representation in April 1945 pleaded the USA to continue eastwards and cross the river Elbe. The decision to halt U.S. Army at Elbe is analyzed in detail in the book The Supreme Command, United States army in World War II, (Washington 1954) by Forrest C Pogue[XXXVII]; and article The liberation of Western Czechoslovakia 1945 by Bryan J Dickerson[XXXVIII]. Both authors concluded that General Eisenhower was under great pressure at that time, liberation of Czechoslovakia was considered lower priority, and the forces tied in Europe were badly needed in Pacific for planned invasion of Japan. The decision to leave establish demarcation line at river Elbe and liberation of Prague was therefore left to the Soviets for purely military reasons.

Forrest C. Pogue concluded that *"political leaders in the United States had framed no policy for dealing with an aggressive Soviet Union in Central Europe. It is equally clear that no political directive was ever issued to General Eisenhower by his American superiors or by the Combined Chiefs of Staff."*

XXXVII Forrest C. Pogue: The Supreme Command, United States Army in World War II, (Washington 1954); Chapter 22. http://www.history.army.mil/books/70-7_22.htm [accessed October 11, 2011]

XXXVIII Bryan J Dickerson: The liberation of Western Czechoslovakia. Military History Online.
http://www.militaryhistoryonline.com/wwii/articles/liberation1945.aspx [accessed October 11, 2011]

On May 10, 1944, The Ministry of Foreign Affairs sent copy this agreement to President Edvard Beneš, Presidium of the Council of Ministries, Ministry of National Defense, Ministry of Finance, Ministry of Trade and Industry, Ministry for Economic Recovery, Ministry of Interior, Ministry of Social Affairs, Ministry of Justice, Ministry of Agriculture, Presidium of the State Council, and the Highest Bureau for Accounting Control. It was obtained from the National Archive in Prague, fund NUKU-L, box 18. The full text is cited below, in original translation from 1944:

Agreement concerning the relationship between the Czechoslovak administration and the Soviet Commander-in-Chief on the entry of Soviet troops into Czechoslovak territory (transcript)

The government of the Czechoslovak Republic and the government of the Union of Soviet Socialist Republics,

Desiring that the relationship between the Czechoslovak Administration n the territory of the Czechoslovak Republic and the Soviet /Allied/ Commander-in-Chief on the entry of Soviet /Allied/ troops into Czechoslovak territory should be adjusted in a spirit of friendship and Alliance existing between the two countries, have agreed the following:

Article 1

As soon as Soviet /Allied/ forces, as the result of war operations, enter Czechoslovak territory, the Soviet /Allied/ Commander-in-Chief will possess the supreme authority and responsibility in all matters essential to the conduct of the war in the zone of war operations for the period necessary to carry out these operations.

Article 2

A Czechoslovak Government delegate for the liberated territories will be appointed, whose task will be:

a/ To set up and direct, in accordance with Czechoslovak law, the administration of the territory which has been cleared of the enemy.

b/ To reconstitute the Czechoslovak armed forces there.

c/ To ensure active co-operation between the Czechoslovak administration and the Soviet /Allied/ Commander-in-Chief, and in particular, to give the local authorities appropriate instructions on the basis of the needs and wishes of the Soviet /Allied/ Commander-in-Chief.

Article 3

The Czechoslovak troops comprised in the Soviet /Allied/ armies when they enter Czechoslovak territory will immediately be utilized there.

Article 4

To ensure contact between the Soviet /Allied/ Commander-in-Chief and the Czechoslovak Government delegate a Czechoslovak military mission will be set up at the headquarters of the Soviet /Allied/ Commander-in-Chief.

Article 5

As regards the zones under the supreme authority of the Soviet /Allied/ Commander-in-Chief, the Czechoslovak Government authorities and representatives in the liberated territory will be in touch with the Soviet /Allied/ Commander-in-Chief through the Czechoslovak Government delegate.

Article 6

As soon as any part of the liberated territory ceases to be a zone of actual war operations, the Czechoslovak Government will take over the full exercise of public authority there and will afford the Soviet /Allied/ Commander-in-Chief co-operation and assistance in all respects through their civilian and military authorities.

Article 7

All members of the Soviet /Allied/ forces on Czechoslovak territory will be amenable to the jurisdiction of the Soviet /Allied/ Commander-in-Chief. All members of the Czechoslovak armed forces will be amenable to the Czechoslovak jurisdiction. Civilians on Czechoslovak territory will likewise be subject to this latter jurisdiction, even in cases of penal offences committed against the Soviet /Allied/ armed forces, unless such offences were committed in the zone of war operations. In the latter case they will come under the jurisdiction of the Soviet Commander-in-Chief. Any doubts about jurisdiction which may arise will be settled by mutual agreement between the Soviet /Allied/ Commander-in-Chief and the Czechoslovak Government delegate.

Article 8

A special agreement will be reached on the subject of financial matters, connected with the entry of Soviet /Allied/ forces into Czechoslovak territory.

Article 9

This agreement comes into force immediately upon its signature. It has been drawn up in duplicate, each copy in the Czechoslovak and the Russian languages.

Both texts are equally authentic.

London, 8th May 1944.

For and on behalf of the government of the Czechoslovak Republic acting Minister of Foreign Affairs Minister of State /signed/ **HUBERT RIPKA**

For and on behalf of the Union of Soviet Socialist Republics, Ambassador extraordinary and plenipotentiary of the Union of Soviet Socialist Republics to the government of the Czechoslovak Republic /signed/ **V LEBEDEV**

Program of Czechoslovak government of the National Front of Czechs and Slovaks adopted on April 5th, 1945, in Košice (Košice Government Program)

This is substantial excerpt from the Košice Government Program, as adopted in April 1945.

Article 1

After more than six years of slavery came time of freedom again. Due to our great ally the Soviet Union, president of the Czechoslovak Republic could return home, and new Czechoslovak government will be formed. New government will be formed by the National Front of Czechs and Slovaks of all political directions and social standings who participated in the national resistance against German tyranny. The new government accepts the task to finish this struggle against German and Hungarian tyranny until achievement of complete freedom. The current government considers its mandate temporary. After liberation of other parts of the Republic and especially Czech lands, the Interim Assembly will meet and confirm the current president in his function until regular elections of the new president. The president will appoint new government with regards to resistance both domestic and in exile. This government then prepares the elections of new General Assembly, which will prepare new Constitution.

Article 2

But there is still fierce resistance in Slovakia where the enemy still has to be defeated. Because the enemy has not yet been defeated in Western Slovakia, the new government will support the Red Army until the final victory. The assistance required by Soviet Union includes repairing of infrastructure, railways, roads, telegraph and phone lines, bridges, and logistical support and accommodation of Red Army personnel, including care of injured Red Army soldiers and food, animal feed, and other material supplies. Political, economic, social, and cultural measures on liberated territory have to be subordinated to the war effort. On liberated territory, the government will continue in mobilization of its citizens and form Czechoslovak army around 1st Czechoslovak Division, take care of prompt training of these units, and their immediate deployment on the frontline. The government will also ensure transfer of Czechoslovak interim armies and air force from the West to the liberated territory. The government will organize national struggle against the occupying force, to ensure their complete and timely expulsion.

Article 3

The government appreciates extraordinary contributions of the Red Army in liberation of Czechoslovakia and wishes to develop cooperation with the Red Army even more. The government intends to shape Czechoslovak, new democratic anti-fascist army per the Red Army's example. To allow close cooperation with the Red Army, re-organization, equipment and training of new Czechoslovak armed forces will be done by Soviet example. The government is fully aware that it is necessary to mobilize national liberation movement on the liberated territories into armed struggle against common enemy. This objective can be fulfilled only with strictly anti-fascist, national-liberation army, army truly democratic, fulfilling the will of the people. New Czechoslovak army will be based on the struggle against Hitlerism, and the main parts of it will be 1st Czechoslovak Army in the USSR, our airmen, Czechoslovak armed division in France, Slovak and Czech guerrilla fighters, and uprising forces in Slovakia. New Czechoslovak army will be built for immediate deployment on the frontline. The newly formed army has to be fully ideologically committed, and for this reason, apolitical character of the army has got to end. To ensure ideological education, the institute of "ideological education" (function known as "politruk") will be introduced. Leading organ in ideological education will report directly to the Ministry of defense. Special attention will be paid to education of young officers and commanding cadres.

The government emphasizes that leadership positions can only be occupied by truly democratic and anti-fascist officers. It is necessary to clean the army from all collaborators and traitors. Inquiries into political reliability of the officers of Czechoslovak army will be performed by military institutions in cooperation with national committees, and the Slovak national council. Responsibility to this belongs to the apparatus of "Defense intelligence" which must be built from the most reliable people.

The government will send as many young officers to Soviet schools as possible. System of ranks will be simplified, and for some there will be also the possibility of designation of a rank or a fast track for the most capable. Both languages, Czech and Slovak, will e treated equally. Service in guerrillas will be recognized as service in Czechoslovak army, and guerrilla fighters will be awarded appropriate ranks upon completion of a short course. The government will introduce new awards and medals.

Article 4

In gratitude to the Soviet Union, Czechoslovak government will coordinate its foreign policy with Soviet Union, as agreed in the bilateral Czech-Soviet Agreement on mutual assistance, friendship, and cooperation, signed on 12 December 1943 (Note: The Christmas Agreement). Soviet Union seeks extension of the agreement to include Poland and form a defence pact against Hitler's Germany. Cooperation with the Soviet Union will be implemented at all levels, including military, economical, political, and cultural in order to secure peaceful development in Czechoslovakia. Czechoslovak representation wishes to participate in mutual exchange of delegates with the Ukrainian Soviet Republic. Czechoslovakia will follow Slavic line of its foreign policy and increase cooperation with Poland, Yugoslavia, and Bulgaria. Czechoslovakia will follow neutral line towards Hungary, after the expulsion of Hungarian invaders and retributions against the collaborators. The same applies to new democratic Austria. Friendly relations with England, USA, and France, are highly valued and should be fostered.

Article 5

In domestic politics, Czechoslovakian politics is based on the will of the people. To secure the people's rights, government will eradicate all fascist elements from the society. National committees formed and elected by the people will control all public affairs. Government will project its power through these committees. All administration institutions and forces formed by previous regimes of invaders and traitors shall be abolished. National Committees shall include people who actively participated in the anti-fascist resistance, and avoid collaborators and traitors. Government will foster creation of other political, social, and cultural organizations, whilst making sure that these are not infiltrated by fascist elements, collaborators, and traitors, and other enemies of the people. Women shall be treated equally in all aspects of political and cultural life.

Article 6

Slovakia is recognized as an independent nation which will be treated as equal with Czechs. Slovakian will form independent state institutions. Common state will be created as defined in the agreement between Slovak National Council and Czechoslovak exile government. Slovaks, who are not subjects to the Presidential Retribution Decrees, will be transferred in the Czechoslovak army. Slovak army will have separate national divisions.

Article 7

Government will cooperate with the Soviet Union in the matter of Ruthenia, as defined by the will of the people *(Note: Ruthenia was seized by the Soviet Union and became part of Ukraine).*

Article 8

Dreadful experiences with German and Hungarian minorities justify measures taken against them after the War. Citizenship rights for these groups will be defined by their political activity during the War. Those sentenced by the Presidential Retribution Decrees will be stripped of Czechoslovak citizenship and expelled from the country. Those who arrived after 1938 will be expelled immediately.

Article 9

Czechoslovak government will prosecute all war criminals, traitors, and collaborators of German and Hungarian oppressors. Hungarians and Germans found guilty will be immediately handed over to **Peoples' Tribunals**. Those who committed crimes against the Allied, especially Soviet forces will be handed over to the Soviet authorities. Special camps will be created for German and Hungarian fascists. **Peoples Tribunals** will be formed to tackle the threat coming from collaborators, fascists, and traitors of Czech and Slovak origin. President **Hácha** and all members of the Beran government who approved the **Berlin Agreement** which was signed on 15 March 1939 will be prosecuted for high treason. The same applies to all members of the Protectorate governments and Slovakian representation. Retributions apply to all pro-fascist journalists, officials and members of pro-Nazi organizations, supporters of the fascists, and pro-Nazi bankers and industrial tycoons. Czechoslovak citizens abroad who betrayed the Republic will be prosecuted the same way. Politicians who were compromised by cooperation with the Nazis will be banned from participation in political activities.

Article 10

National management will be imposed on the property of traitors, collaborators, and expelled Germans and Hungarians (Note: = confiscation of private property). Private property will be secured by National Committees, until a decision by the relevant authority is made.

Article 11

Land of traitors, collaborators and fascists will be nationalized without compensation, and its administration will be given to the newly established National Land Fund. Confiscation of property will be performed by National Committees with the assistance of Agrarian Commissions. Confiscated land will then be redistributed to those Czechs, Slovaks, and Ukrainians, who participated in anti-fascist resistance (note: non-communist resistance is not considered here), **and to the victims of the Nazi terror. Payment for this land should not exceed value of 1 to 2 year harvest. In some cases, this fee can be waved.**

Article 12

Strategic industries have to be rebuilt with the highest priority, to revive the economy. This includes energy sector, mining industry, water supplies, communications, roads and railways, and food and food processing industry. Businesses should be granted easy access to credit, and all financial institutions should be rebuilt. Any assistance available from other Allies, such as UNRRA and Lend lease agreement, shall be used as much as possible.

Article 13

All land has to be used for production of food, with no regards to the ownership structure. Government in cooperation with agricultural organizations will define compulsory production norms which will have to be met. This production will be sold at fixed prices. Any extra production can be sold on a free market.

Article 14

Government will guarantee equal pay for women and socially disadvantaged persons. Welfare system will be funded from state budget. Castles and mansions will be nationalized to benefit the people, especially those who participated in the national struggle for independence, and the disadvantaged. Intelligentsia will be invited to rebuild the country with no political preferences. All workers will have a right to voluntarily participate in trade unions and factory committees and elect their own officials.

Article 15

Schools and other cultural institutions, such as theatres, libraries, etc, will be cleared from fascist elements, and all textbooks published during the Protectorate era will be removed. Similar cleansing will occur in journalism, broadcasting, and film. All German and Hungarian schools will be closed. Czech and Slovak schools closed during the Nazi regime will be re-opened, and speedy graduation will be allowed to those who were expelled from Nazi institutions. Students will be encouraged to enter technical scientific fields and their acceptance on technical schools will be facilitated. Slovakian cultural institutions will be independent from Czech ones. Slavic orientation of Czech and Slovak culture will be supported. German and Hungarian influence will be eliminated. Cultural relations to the USSR will be fostered by the government; all anti-Soviet elements will be removed, and the youth will be educated about the state establishment, development, economy, and culture of the Soviet Union. Russian language will be prioritized in new teaching plans. Universities will teach new subjects such as Soviet history, Soviet economics, and Soviet law.

Agreement of the governments of Czechoslovak Republic and the USSR from November 23, 1945, and Protocol on mining of uranium ore in CSR and supplies to the USSR

Source: František Lepka: Czech Uranium. Unknown economical and political context 1945-2002

Strictly confidential (declassified)

AGREEMENT

Between the government of the USSR and the government of Czechoslovakia on expansion of mining of ore and concentrates in Czechoslovakia which contain radium and other radioactive elements and their supplies to the USSR. The government of the USSR and the CSR agreed on the following:

Part 1

Czechoslovak government organizes a state enterprise for the research and exploitation of all deposits containing radium and other radioactive elements which belong to the Czechoslovak state.

Part 2

Czechoslovak government will do everything to maximize the increase of mining of ore and concentrates containing radium and other radioactive elements in the district of town Jáchymov.

Part 3

The government of the USSR will provide all technical assistance for research and exploitation of above mentioned deposits. This assistance will comprise of sending professionals for organization of research and industrial exploration of deposits and for works in mining of ore and concentrates, and also of supply of necessary equipment and materials.

Part 4

Both governments will form a permanent Czechoslovak-Soviet Commission with headquarters in Prague, consisting of four members (two of each government). Assignment of the committee is as follows:

a) To elaborate directives in order to expand geological-exploration works and increase mining of ore and concentrates.

b) To work out plans of mining of ore and concentrates; whilst the basic plans have to be prepared in time for the period of at least 5 years with gradual increase of the plan providing the results of geological exploration give basis to this.

c) Solving of all questions which arise as a result of fulfilling the agreement on technical assistance and supplies.

d) To set prices for the ore and concentrates and for radium in line with paragraph 5 of this agreement based on own expenses and adding a normal percentage of profit.

The commission conducts its activities by statutes it sets up. The decisions of the commission are valid as long as both sides agree. In case the Czechoslovak and Soviet members of the commission fail to reach an agreement, the matter will be resolved directly by both governments.

Part 5

With regards to paragraph 4, the Czechoslovak-Soviet commission will decide what part of the extracted ore and concentrate will remain in Czechoslovakia for its economical and scientific needs. All remaining extracted ore and concentrates containing radium and other radioactive elements will be given to the USSR, whilst 50% of radium will be after processing in the USSR returned back to CSR, providing this comes from the ore and concentrates provided by the CSR for processing in the USSR.

Mutual settlements resulting from delivered ore and concentrates for processing in the USSR and return of radium to Czechoslovakia, will be conducted based on prices for ore, concentrates, and radium, set in agreement of both governments, with paying the arising differences in supplies of goods or in foreign currency as per agreement of the high covenant parties.

Part 6

The Soviet side agrees to send among professionals to Czechoslovakia one professional technical director, one professional highly skilled leading engineer, and one master of technical control for the Jáchymov facility.

Part 7

Both sides concur that they will exchange scientific knowledge concerning usage of ore and concentrates containing radium and radioactive elements.

Part 8

This agreement comes in effect immediately after signature and is valid for 20 years.

Drawn up in Prague on November 23, 1945, in two authentic copies, in Czech and Russian languages, whilst both texts have the same validity

Based on authorization by the government of the Czechoslovak Republic **H Ripka**

Based on authorization by the government of the USSR **I Bakulin**

PROTOCOL

To the agreement between the government of the Czechoslovak Republic and the government of the USSR on expansion of mining of ore and concentrates in Czechoslovakia containing radium and other radioactive elements, as well as on their supplies to the USSR. In relation to today's signing of the agreement in Prague between the government of the Czechoslovak Republic and the government of the USSR on expansion of mining of ore and concentrates in Czechoslovakia containing radium and other radioactive elements as well as on their supplies to the USSR, the following agreement was reached:

1) From the total amount of the extracted ore and concentrates containing radium and other radioactive elements for the period of first 5 years of validity of the cited agreement, 10% of these ores will remain in Czechoslovakia for its economical and scientific needs.

2) The government of the Czechoslovak Republic will provide appropriate rooms in Jáchymov and in Prague according to the needs of the Soviet members of the Czechoslovak-Soviet commission.

3) In order to ensure confidentiality of the mining of ore and concentrates containing radium and other radioactive elements and their supplies to the USSR, the Czechoslovak-Soviet commission will determine corresponding regulations for Jáchymov and possible other sites in the Czechoslovak Republic.

4) The abovementioned agreement between the Czechoslovak government and the USSR is strictly confidential.

Drawn up in Prague on November 23, 1945, in two copies, in Czech and Russian languages, whilst both texts have the same validity.

Based on authorization by the respective governments signed by **H Ripka** (Czechoslovakia) and **I Bakulin** (USSR)

Analysis Background to Czechoslovak Crisis by former U.S. Ambassador to Czechoslovakia Laurence A Steinhardt for General Marshall, U.S. Secretary of State, from April 30, 1948. ^{XXXIX}

860F.00/4-3048

The Ambassador in Czechoslovakia (Steinhardt) to the Secretary of State

PRAHA, April 30, 1948

SECRET No.309

Sir:

1. I have the honor to supplement the Embassy's coverage of the Czechoslovak Government crisis of February 1948 by certain descriptive and analytical comments.

2. A crisis such as developed in February 1948 was probably inherent in the situation ever since the consummation of the Czechoslovak-Soviet Treaty of Friendship and Military alliance of December 12, 1943. An understanding of the causes of this alliance requires a brief look into the historical and psychological background of the Czechoslovak nation.

3. The Czechs are a little people. Situated in the geographical center of Europe, they have for centuries been the focusing point for economic and political tensions resulting in countless wars and in successive waves of emigration. The high point in their history occurred in 1346-1378 which was due to the triple coincidence of the strong and constructive personality of King Charles IV (who also became Holy Roman Emperor), the discovery of large silver deposits, and the discovery of large silver deposits, and the temporary absence of other strong political forces in Europe. Such a situation did not occur again until 1918 when another power vacuum in Europe and the strong personality of Thomas G. Masaryk caused the emergence of Czechoslovakia as a State. A wave of emigration followed the destructive Hussite wars of 1415-1436. Another wave followed the outbreak of the Thirty Years War in 1620 which began a 300-year domination by the Hapsburgs. Emigration to America occurred toward the end of the 19th century. Finally World War II eliminated first

the Jewish business elements and then the 2,500,000 Sudeten Germans who were the industrial backbone of the country.

4. These waves of emigration repeatedly drained off the cream of the population, leaving a residue of small farmers and artisans who have never seem able to exercise firmness, courage and noble traits in time of crisis but rather have chosen to bow to political storms which have raged about the country. These people have preferred to survive without undue struggle rather than to fight for their freedom. Under the 300 years of Hapsburg domination which ended in 1918 the Czechs developed an ingrained genius for subtle opposition to the existing regime. They are much more adapt when in opposition than when they themselves are in control and faced with the problems of construction and positive rule of which they have in modern times had only twenty years of experience.

5. In the chronic state of being a "little people", the Czechs have always needed strong allies for survival. The devious mental characteristics just described have caused them to attempt to play off their neighbors against each other, to indulge in double-talk (for example the statements of Jan Masaryk during the past two years), and to place bets on both sides. This method was successful in World War II when they escaped destruction, gained in industrial strength and emerged on the winning side. However, their alliance with Russia combined with the present aggressive Soviet political policy in Europe has prevented the Czechs from "having it both ways" as the recent crisis demonstrated. Their occasional ability to play off one side against anther has given them a bargaining position and an unwarranted sense of importance. At present as a people they are correspondingly deflated.

6. The Czechs have had bad experiences with their allies. The French and British deserted them at Munich 1938. Our great mistake in waging a purely military war while the Soviet Union was waging a combined military and political struggle obviously contributed to our loss of influence in Central and Eastern Europe. The Czechs are firmly of the opinion that e "wrote them off" or, in other words, "consigned them to the Soviet sphere of influence" in 1943. While there may have been no formal exchanges on this subject, our later actions indicated the correctness of this belief in the eyes of the Czechs. President Beneš received a polite but non-committal reception in Washington early in 1943. The Tehran Conference followed in November. What Stalin may have told Beneš in December about spheres of influence and "All-Slav

Brotherhood" may easily be imagined. In any event, there was no alternative than for the Czechs to sign with the Soviets. Our attitude at Yalta and Potsdam on boundaries and repatriations and especially the halting of our army in May 1945, thus permitting Soviet forces to liberate Praha confirmed our stand in the minds of the Czechs. Hindsight now indicates that further attention by us to the political aspects of the war might have given us control of Central Europe at a nominal cost.

7. The Soviet-Czechoslovak alliance of December 12, 1943, doubtless prevented temporarily a post-war situation in Czechoslovakia such as developed in Poland. It offered Czechoslovakia tangible benefits only so long as the Soviet Union chose to abstain from an aggressive European policy. Since the Soviets in fact continued to be aggressive, it was only a matter of time before a crisis would come in February, May, August or the next year was partly a matter of opportunity but was fundamentally a Moscow decision. Nearly all Czechoslovak authorities believed no crisis was imminent in February since it was to the advantage of the Soviet Union to keep the situation calm in Czechoslovakia in order to continue the flow of materials to the Soviet Union. This fact, according to Dr Hubert Ripka, Minister of Foreign Trade, after his return from Moscow in December 1947, was fully understood by Soviet Economic Commissar Mikoyan[1] and other high Soviet officials. The benefit of hindsight indicates that the Czechoslovak non-Communist Cabinet members did not realize the extent to which the country would be utilized as a pawn in the Soviet over-all plan for Europe. It is evident that a decision was reached in Moscow that political considerations outweighed the possible economic disadvantages to the Soviet Union of a comparatively early "putsch" in Czechoslovakia. Furthermore, the resignations of twelve non-Communist Ministers created a vacuum and the Communists moved in. Although the Communists did not precipitate the crisis (although they doubtless planned to do so), they took full advantage of it just as they did at Bogota.[2]

8. It is now clear that the decision of the twelve ministers, representing the National Socialists, Catholics and Slovak Democrats, to resign was taken with direct encouragement and consent of President

---

[1]   Anastas Ivanovich Mikoyan, Soviet Minister for Foreign Trade

[2]   Reference to the abortive revolution in Bogota, Columbia, in early April 1948; for documentation on the concern of the United States over the events in Bogota, see index entry, Columbia: Civil disturbances in volume IX.

Beneš. During the five days these resignations were pending and not accepted, there are definite records that the President was approached at least four times by either the Ministers or their representatives with a view to strengthening him in withholding his consent to accepting the resignations. While the techniques employed have now proven incorrect, it seems clear that the debacle which followed may largely be attributable to weakness on the part of the President which is hardly excusable on the grounds of his sub-normal physical health.

9. As to the extent of Soviet interference and intimidation, it is now clear that President Beneš was greatly frightened by the Soviet specter. There are continued reports that pressure brought upon the President by Gottwald and the Trade Union representatives and their adherents who marched on the castle caused the President to fear internal strife and the consequent necessity by Soviet troops in surrounding countries to come in "restore order". There was no evidence of any Soviet troop concentrations on the borders of Czechoslovakia. It also appears that the extent of the Soviet threats was probably less than on similar recent occasions in Finland and Iran, both of which countries successfully resisted such threats whereas the Czechs succumbed to them. While the conduct of the Czechs in this respect is not condoned, it can partly be explained by their historical background outlined above. Furthermore, during the crisis, there was a terrific amount of dashing around by the various Ministers and high Government officials, to watch what each of them was doing, to attempt to keep them firm in their previous pledges, to prevent minor members of the non-Communist parties from succumbing to Communist blandishments. In short, there was a great deal of distrust, lack of unity, loose talk and physical movement, all of which caused indecision and lack of positive action on the part of the moderate forces. Of this, the Communists took full advantage.

10. There was no direct evidence of Soviet interference. Even the activities of Soviet ambassador Zorin, who arrived in Prague by airplane on February 19, cannot be placed under the heading of direct interference. Those of his conversations of which the Embassy has creditable reports were opened by a discussion of the grain situation. In one case, he is known to have avoided the discussion of politics at least until he left the office of the Cabinet Minister on whom he was calling. In some cases, he discussed politics with the office personnel who were Communists. Zorin is not a forceful, door-slamming type and his activities are not comparable to those of Vishinsky in Bucharest during the crisis

there.[3XLII] The only indications of definite preparation which may have had Soviet aid are that the Communists' "Action Committees" sprang into the picture with great suddenness on the morning of February 23 and that in a special demonstration about the same date Trade Union militia appeared on the public squares with new rifles. It had long been known that the Trade Union groups had possessed caches of arms in various factories which dated back to the 1945 Revolution, most of the arms having originated from underground sources during the war period. However, the presence of brand new rifles with shiny unvarnished butts took most people by surprise. The Action Committees were obviously well organized by the Communists. In essence this is a well known Czech institution which has existed since the war, national committees which exercise much local influence having existed ever since May 1945 originating also from the wartime underground movement. The action Committees were simply a new name for an old phenomenon to which the Czechs are well accustomed but they may well have been directly encouraged by Soviet support.

11. As to the death of Foreign Minister Masaryk on the night of March 9-10, 1948, the actual circumstances are still surrounded by mystery. It is possible that definite evidence may be obtained to determine whether it was in fact suicide or murder. The suicide theory is the only one which the Government could officially announce and the fact that the official announcement was not made until at least six hours after his death indicates that higher Czech officialdom was caught by surprise. This would indicate that in case it was murder, the deed was perpetrated by non-Czech persons. As reported by the Embassy, there are several circumstances which would tend to support the murder theory but the Embassy is still inclined to give credence to the suicide theory in the absence of further facts. More that three-fourths of the Czech population believes in the murder theory which is of course embarrassing to the Communists. Certain unpublished statements which come from the President's immediate entourage and recently reported by the Embassy, to the effect that opened razor blades and knotted pajama cords were

---

[3]   In late February 1945 the then Assistant People's Commissar for Foreign Affairs of the Soviet Union Andrey Yanuaryevich Vyshinsky took a direct hand in persuading King Michael of Romania to agree to the appointment of a Communist-dominated cabinet. For documentation on the efforts of the United States to help bring about the establishment of democracy in Romania, see Foreign relations, 1945, vol. V, pp. 464 ff.

found in Masaryk's bedroom, give credence to the theory of premeditated suicide. The sources have suppressed this information because they desire the public for the present to keep on thinking that it was murder. Masaryk's death of course created a wide-spread feeling of sorrow among the population. The Communist elements heavily played up the deprecatory messages which Masaryk had received from his friends in the West as one of the causes of his suicide. Regardless of whether it was suicide or murder, his death retrieved his reputation which had rapidly dwindled during the February crisis. Furthermore, from a political viewpoint, it made very little difference whether it was suicide or murder since the net result was to indicate that his continuance in office was inconsistent with the basic philosophy and with that of his distinguished father. He realized too late that he could not look in two directions at the same time.

12. The Communists were aggressive and bold, and were sufficiently organized to take advantage of the situation. The non-Communists had no adhesion as a group, did not recognize the issue as one of Communism against non-Communism and continued to place their individual party loyalties and personal ambitions ahead of their opposition to Communism. This, combined with weak leadership at the top, particularly on the part of the President, caused the debacle. From the American viewpoint, it seems despicable that, with the exception of a few students, not a single person from the President of the Republic down to the humblest citizen even uttered a public word in defense of their political liberties. Several Czechs, friendly to the Embassy, have since stated privately that since their people were not willing to fight for their freedom, they do not deserve to have it. Many people who hold such beliefs have subsequently fled from the country and are now attempting to form a resistance movement in exile. This also fits into the historical pattern and reduces to zero any possibility of effective resistance at present to Communism within Czechoslovakia itself. Such resistance is out of the question since Czechoslovakia is now completely a police state.

13. At the present date (April 30, 1948) the country has experienced its first wave of arrests and ejection of "reactionaries" from their jobs. A period of comparative calm has ensued. This enables the Communists to consolidate their position. The elections now scheduled for the end of May no longer have important significance since voters only have a choice between the single Government list and a blank ballot. No party is giving the Communists any opposition and it seems probable that all non-

Communist parties will either soon be dissolved or united with the Communists. Czechoslovakia has become a full-fledged puppet state. Rumors are in circulation that it may soon be integrated legally with the Soviet Union, a development which could quite possibly occur. At any rate, the next wave of arrests is likely to eliminate any remaining "reactionaries" and in the opinion of some, even certain of the milder Communists. The higher officials are taking extra precautions for their personal safety.

14. While there is a great deal of grumbling and persons friendly to the West state that as high as 80% of the population, including some Communists, are highly dissatisfied with what has happened, it is not in the Czechoslovak character to offer resistance or to take effective counter action. There are many people who believe that their only salvation will be in a war between the United States and the Soviet Union. They do not think of the disastrous physical results such a war might have in their country. They are in the shameful position of not having raised voice or hand against the communist domination but at the same time they hope for the United States to come and save them. This mentality results partly from their experience during World War II when the country succeeded in sitting out the war with practically no physical destruction and survived in better economic state than it previously enjoyed. Therefore, those who remain in the country look forward to another conflict in which they might enjoy similar benefits and at the end be able to make a good case for being on the winning side, whichever that may be. While this estimate is highly deprecatory and possibly unjust to a few high-minded Czechs, it is intended to describe the general thinking of the country. In case of a future conflict, there will doubtless be a considerable reservoir of latent good will in Czechoslovakia toward the United States. This will express itself in some obstructionism on the part of people against the Soviet occupiers. To put it the other way, no effective benefit to the anti-Soviet belligerents can be expected without the presence of ground forces within the country.

15. As to our policy toward the puppet Czechoslovak Government, it is obvious that we should render it no material or moral support whatever. To do so would be diametrically opposed to United States interests. The only justification for the continuance of diplomatic representation is for the maintenance of the existing small, mutually advantageous trade and for the convenience of Americans visiting Czechoslovakia. Our radio broadcasts to Czechoslovakia continue to have

a limited usefulness which may yield distant rather than immediate returns. The Czechoslovak political exiles could for the present be utilized in this project and also as lecturers and for obtaining covert political intelligence. As a group they would probably fall to political bickering unless we took a direct hand in organizing them. Within a few weeks the possibilities for obtaining open political intelligence in Czechoslovakia will undoubtedly be greatly reduced, and consequently plans should be made for increased covert activities in this part of Europe.

16. The benefit of hindsight indicates that Certain measures could have been taken which might have delayed the Communist domination of Czechoslovakia. These are listed as of possible application in other countries where similar situations prevail.

a. An increase in our radio and other propaganda services including publication of the full story of why we permitted Soviet forces to liberate Berlin and Praha. The smallest and most impoverished countries spend large sums for this purpose whereas we greatly reduced ours in 1947.

b. Negotiation of treaties of commerce and cultural agreements. Small countries are flattered by such attentions.

c. Assistance in the form of much needed commodities on a sale (not gift) basis. The Soviet Union came to Czechoslovakia's rescue after the 1947 drought by *selling* needed grain at a high price.

d. Direct internal interference for the purpose of organizing the existing anti-Communist forces effectively. The latter are usually more numerous. Since they normally lack organizing ability they are totally lost to us if we do not mobilize them. This is contrary to conventional diplomacy but we have an opponent who breaks the rules.

Only the first of the above measures would any longer be of utility in Czechoslovakia. These techniques have proven effective when used by the Soviets, while at the same time they try to turn to their own advantage what they regard as our soft idealism, our conventional "fair-play" methods and our attempts to "buy" good will. Greater use by us of soviet methods might result in both positive and preventative benefits.

Respectfully yours,

LAURENCE A. STEINHARDT

BIBLIOGRAPHY

Books:

Andrew C, Gordievsky O: ***Comrade Kryuchkov's Instructions:*** Top Secret Files on KGB Foreign Operations, 1975-1985. Stanford University Press (February 1, 1994)

Andrew C, Gordievsky O: ***KGB: The Inside Story of Its Foreign Operations from Lenin to Gorbachev***. Harpercollins; 1st edition (May 1992)

Andrew C, Gordievsky O: ***More Instructions from the Centre: Top Secret Files on KGB Global Operations 1975-1985***. Routledge; 1 edition (April 30, 1992)

Andrew C, Mitrokhin V: ***The Mitrokhin Archive The Sword and the Shield:*** The Mitrokhin Archive and the Secret History of the KGB. Basic Books (September 5, 2000).

Andrew C, Mitrokhin V: ***World was going our way.*** Basic Books 2005.

Andrew C: ***Defend the Realm: The authorized history of MI5***, page 250-253; Knopf 2009.

August F, Beneš J: ***Ve znamení temna: sovětská špionážní a podvratná činnost proti Československu v letech 1918-1969***, Votobia, 2001 (original: Indiana University)

Barron J: ***Mig Pilot: The Final Escape of Lieutenant Belenko.*** Mcgraw-Hill; First Edition edition (February 1980)

Beneš J: ***Zločin genocidy.*** Votobia 2001.

Beneš, J: ***Čas voněl snem.*** Primus 2005.

Bertaux D, Thompson P: ***International Yearbook of oral history and life stories, Volume II, Between Generations: Family models, myths and memories.*** Oxford University Press 1993.

Brown A: ***Airmen in exile.*** Sutton Publishing, 2000.

Česká Národní Rada: ***Armáda a národ.*** Nakladatelství Mazáč 1938.

Clayton A Oliver: ***Survivor's Guide to the Czech Republic. An unofficial setting sourcebook for Twilight 2013.*** http://web.mac.com/c_oliver/2013/Survivors_Guide_to_the_Czech_Republic.pdf. [accessed October 14, 2011]

Courtois S, Werth N, Panne JL, Paczkowskij A, Bartošek K, Margolin JL: ***Černá kniha komunismu – zločiny, terror, represe I, II.*** (Black book of communism; Crimes, terror, repressions I, II). Paseka 1999.

Dahl RA: ***What political institutions does large scale democracy require?*** The meaning of American democracy; Academy of Political Science, 2005.

Douglass J: ***Betrayed.*** 1st Book Library (June 14, 2002).

Douglass J: *Red Cocaine: The drugging of America.* Second Opinion Pub Inc; First Edition (1990)

Frolík J: *Špión vypovídá.* Orbis 1990.

Hejl, V: *Zpráva o organizovaném násilí* (Report on organized violence). Univerzum 1990.

Kvaček R, Kuklík J, Mandelová H, Pařízková I: *"XX. Století o sobě. Dějiny v dokumentech;"* Dialog 2005.

Lockwood JS, Lockwood KO: *Russian view of US strategy, Its Past, its future.* Transaction Publishers, 1993.

Masin B: *Gauntlet.* Naval Institute Press; 2006.

Moore, DT: *Critical thinking and intelligence analysis.* National Defense Intelligence College, Mar 2007. http://www.ndic.edu/press/2641.htm [accessed October 14, 2011]

Moravec F: *Špión jemuž neveřili.* Academia 2002.

National Defense Intelligence College: *Interrogation, World War II, Vietnam, and Iraq.* NDIC Press 2008. http://www.ndic.edu/press/12010.htm [accessed October 13, 2011]

Oxford Biography Index entry: *Karel Janoušek (1893–1971), officer in the Czech air force.* http://www.oxforddnb.com/index/93/101093047/ [accessed October 14, 2011]

Phillips John T., II: *George Washington's Rules of Civility: Complete With the Original French Text and New French-To-English Translations* (The Complete George Washington Series, Vol. 1); Goose Creek Productions; Collector's edition (November 30, 2003)

Pipes R: *Russia under the new regime.* Penguin Non-classics, 1997.

Pogue, Forrest C: *The Supreme Command, United States Army in World War II,* (Washington 1954); Chapter 22. http://www.history.army.mil/books/70-7_22.htm [accessed October 11, 2011]

Pospisil J: *Hyeny v akci,* Lípa, Vizovice 2003. http://knihy.abz.cz/prodej/hyeny-v-akci [accessed October 14, 2011]

Pospisil J: *Hyeny,* Lípa Vizovice 2002; http://knihy.abz.cz/prodej/hyeny [accessed October 14, 2011]

Rozhoň, František: *Příběh revoluce* (The story of revolution). Full text at website Svědomí (Conscience):
http://www.svedomi.cz/pribehy/rof_ceskoslovensko_pribeh_revoluce.htm#r_maffi epripravilavskutkusametovourevoluci [accessed October 13, 2011]

Šedivý ZF: *Světlana. I. CSL. partyzánská brigáda Jana Žižky z Trocnova ve třetím odboji.* Published by Papyrus, 1997.

Šejna J: *We will bury you.* Sidgwick & Jackson (August 1985)

Shapiro, RY: *The meaning of American Democracy.* The Academy of political science, 2005.

Stalin JV: *Economic problems of socialism in the USSR*, published in USSR in 1952; published in Beijing in 1972; http://www.marx2mao.com/PDFs/EPS52.pdf [accessed October 14, 2011]

Suvorov V: *Inside the aquarium - Making a top Soviet spy.* MacMillan 1985.

Vachalovský P, Bok J: *Špión vypovídá II.* J. W. Hill, 2000. Original from the University of Michigan.

Vitas RA: *United States and Lithuania. The Stimson Doctrine of non-recognition.* Praeger Publishers, 1990.

Walker, Andrew: *Nazi War Trials.* Pocket Essentials Series; November 2005.

Government publications

CIA: *The CIA and Strategic Warning: The 1968 Soviet-Led Invasion of Czechoslovakia.* An overview. http://www.foia.cia.gov/CzechInvasion/8-StrategicWarning/2009-09-01.pdf [accessed October 17, 2011]

Czech Government office: *Národní Bezpečnostní Strategie České Republiky, 2003*; Czech version:
http://www.vlada.cz/assets/ppov/brs/dokumenty/bezpecnostni_strategie_2003.pdf [accessed October 15, 2011]; and English (web of Czech Ministry of Foreign Affairs in Berlin):
http://www.mzv.cz/berlin/de/informationen_uber_tschechien/politik/aussenpoliti k/sicherheitsstrategie_der_tschechischen/index.html [accessed October 15, 2011]

Czech Ministry of Defense: *National Security Strategy of the Czech Republic, September   2011.*
http://www.mocr.army.cz/images/id_8001_9000/8503/Czech_Security_Strategy_2 011.pdf [accessed October 15, 2011]

Czech Ministry of Foreign Affairs: *The Military strategy of the Czech Republic. Prague 2008*. http://merln.ndu.edu/whitepapers/Czech_Republic_English-2008.pdf [accessed October 15, 2011]

Doyle C: *Extraterritorial application of US Criminal Law.* Congressional Research Service, March 2010. http://www.fas.org/sgp/crs/misc/94-166.pdf [accessed October 15, 2011]

DTIRP: *Implementing missile defense in Europe.* September 15, 2011; DTIRP. http://dtirp.dtra.mil/NC/displayArticle.aspx?displayFile=G/g_15sep11.htm [accessed October 15, 2011]

Hildreth Steven A, Ek Carl: *Long-range ballistic missile defense in Europe.* Congressional Research Service, 2009.
http://www.fas.org/sgp/crs/weapons/RL34051.pdf [accessed October 15, 2011]

ICISS: *IC R2P Responsibility to Protect.* Report of the International Commission on intervention and state sovereignty. December 2001. http://responsibilitytoprotect.org/ICISS%20Report.pdf [accessed October 15, 2011]

Institute for study of totalitarian regimes: *Newly published documents obtained from Ukraine on invasion 1968.* http://www.ustrcr.cz/cs/dokumenty-kgb [accessed October 14, 2011]

JPRS Report: JPRS-TAC-91-019; *Arms Control.* July 24, 1991; *President Havel Signs CFE Instruments of Ratification* [CTK 22 Jul] 5; http://www.dtic.mil/cgi-bin/GetTRDoc?Location=U2&doc=GetTRDoc.pdf&AD=ADA345466 [accessed October 17, 2011]

JPRS Report: JPRS-TAC-91-019; August 8, 1991; *Arms Control.* July 24, 1991; **Chief of Staff: CSFR SS-23's Not Covered by INF Treaty** [CTK 27 Jul]. http://www.dtic.mil/cgi-bin/GetTRDoc?Location=U2&doc=GetTRDoc.pdf&AD=ADA345466 [accessed October 17, 2011]

JPRS Report: Circumstances surrounding Pavel Wonka's death reexamined. Foreign Broadcast Information Service: JPRS Report; Aug 20, 1990. http://dodreports.com/pdf/ada372752.pdf [accessed October 14, 2011]

Library of Congress, Federal Research Division, *Country studies: Czechoslovakia.* http://lcweb2.loc.gov/frd/cs/soviet_union/su_appn.html [accessed October 14, 2011].

Library of Congress: *Early history of Czechoslovakia:* http://www.loc.gov/rr/european/imsk/slovakia.html [accessed October 12, 2011]

Mlsna, P, Šlehofer L, Urban D: *The paths of Czech Constitutionality. On the 90th anniversary of the passage of the first Czechoslovak Constitution.* Government Office, 2010. http://www.vlada.cz/assets/udalosti/vystavy/Cesty-ceske-ustavnosti.pdf [accessed October 12, 2011]

NSA: Document No. 81: *Transcript of Leonid Brezhnev's Telephone Conversation with Alexander Dubček, August 13, 1968.* The Prague Spring Foundation. Available at http://www.gwu.edu/~nsarchiv/nsa/publications/DOC_readers/psread/doc81.htm [accessed June 4, 2011]

ORS: *The British Constitution and Monarchy. Public affairs for journalists 2009;* Online Resource Centre. Full text of the document is available at http://www.oup.com/uk/orc/bin/9780199552610/morrison_ch01.pdf [accessed October 12, 2011]

Praha.eu: *Short story of the invitation letter.* http://www.praha.eu/jnp/en/extra/Year_68/august/short_story_of_the_invitation_letter.html [accessed October 14, 2011]

Steinhardt, L: *Attitude of the United States with respect to the Czechoslovak governmental crisis of February 1948 and its aftermath.*

http://images.library.wisc.edu/FRUS/EFacs/1948v04/reference/frus.frus1948v04.i0
007.pdf [accessed on October 12, 2011]

US State Department: *Remarks to the Press on Release of Purportedly
Confidential Documents by Wikileaks* (November 29, 2010).
http://www.state.gov/secretary/rm/2010/11/152078.htm [accessed October 15,
2011].

U.S. Army: *Ranger handbook. Not for the weak, not for the faint-hearted.* U.S.
Army SH 21-76; Ranger training brigade, United States Army Infantry School, Fort
Benning, Georgia. July 2006.

Government publications – Legal norms

Constitution of the United States of America
http://www.usconstitution.net/const.html [accessed on October 12, 2011]

Constitution of the Third French Republic
http://www.assemblee-nationale.fr/histoire/constitution-troisieme-republique.asp
[accessed October 12, 2011]

Constitution of Switzerland
http://www.admin.ch/ch/e/rs/1/101.en.pdf [accessed October 12, 2011]

Constitution of the Austrian-Hungarian Empire from 1867
http://cs.wikipedia.org/wiki/Prosincov%C3%A1_%C3%BAstava [accessed October
12, 2011]

The Interim Constitution, Czechoslovakia, 1918 Act 37/1918
http://www.psp.cz/docs/texts/constitution_1918.html [accessed October 12, 2011]

Constitutional Act 121/1920, Czechoslovakia
http://www.psp.cz/docs/texts/constitution_1920.html [accessed October 12, 2011]

Constitutional Act 57/1946, Czechoslovakia
http://www.psp.cz/docs/laws/dek/u1946.html [accessed October 12, 2011]

Constitutional Act 213/1948, Czechoslovakia. Original as obtained from the
Museum of Third Resistance (English translation):
http://www.anticomm.co.uk/?p=1023 [accessed October 14, 2011]

Act 231/1948, Czechoslovakia – Act on Protection of People's Democratic
Republic, §52. Original text in Czech
http://aplikace.mvcr.cz/archiv2008/sbirka/1948/sb85-48.pdf [Accessed on October
14, 2011]

Constitutional Act 150/1948 (May 9, 1948), Czechoslovakia
http://www.psp.cz/docs/texts/constitution_1948.html [accessed October 13, 2011]

Constitutional Act 100/1960 (July 11, 1960), Czechoslovak Socialist Republic
http://www.psp.cz/docs/texts/constitution_1960.html [accessed October 13]

Constitutional Act 1/1993, (December 1992), Czech Republic
http://www.psp.cz/docs/laws/constitution.html [accessed October 12, 2011]

Act 198/1993 – Act on unlawfulness of the communist regime, Czech Republic http://www.sds.cz/docs/prectete/ezakon/198_1993.htm [accessed October 14, 2011]

Meritorious President Beneš Act 292/2004.
http://iuridictum.pecina.cz/w/Lex_Bene%C5%A1 [accessed October 15, 2011]

International agreements and treaties, founding agreements

Cleveland Agreement, 1915, (published informally)
http://www.moderni-dejiny.cz/danek-clevelandska-dohoda-22-23-10-1915-108/ [accessed October 12, 2011]

Pittsburgh Agreement, 1918, (published informally)
http://www.waymarking.com/waymarks/WMAZPN_The_1918_Pittsburgh_Agreement_MRStefanik_memorial_Bratislava_Slovakia. [accessed October 12, 2011]

The Washington Declaration: 1918, (published informally)
http://www.just.wz.cz/view.php?cislodanku=2006071303 [accessed October 12, 2011]

Saint Germain-en-Laye Agreement, 1920, (section III, Articles 53-58):
http://www.austlii.edu.au/au/other/dfat/treaties/1920/3.html [accessed October 12, 2011]

Saint Germain-en-Laye Agreement, 1920, (Naval History)
http://navalhistory.flixco.info/H/181013/8330/a0.htm [accessed October 12, 2011].

Munich Pact, 1938, (published informally)
http://jirikkucera.files.wordpress.com/2011/03/mc3bcnchner-abkommen1.pdf [accessed October 12, 2011]

Munich Pact, 1938, (Yale Law School Library)
English translation. Yale Law School, Lillian Goldman Law Library, The Avalon Project: http://avalon.law.yale.edu/imt/munich1.asp [accessed October 12, 2011]

Hitler's Decree 75/1939 on the establishment of Protectorate Böhmen und Mahren, 1939, (published informally)
http://www.fronta.cz/dokument/hitleruv-vynos-o-zrizeni-protektoratu-cechy-a-morava [accessed October 12, 2011]

Tehran conference: November 28 to December 1, 1943, (Yale Law School Library)
The Avalon Project, Yale Law School:
http://www.yale.edu/lawweb/avalon/wwii/tehran.htm [accessed October 14, 2011]

Treaty on friendship, mutual assistance, and post-war cooperation between Czechoslovak Republic and the USSR signed in Moscow on December 12, 1943. The agreement was published in February 1946 by a Notice of the Ministry of Interior, and is cited in Appendix.

Agreement concerning the relationship between the Czechoslovak government and the Soviet Commander in Chief on the entry of Soviet troops into Czechoslovak territory, London May 8, 1944, (National Archive, Prague)

Copy of the agreement in both Czech and English versions was obtained from the National Archive in Prague, fund NUKU-L (The Highest Accounting Control Bureau London), box No 18; and is cited in Appendix.

Agreements concerning prisoners of war and civilians liberated by forces operating under United States Command: Crimea (Yalta) 11 Feb 1945. FO 371/47896. United States interpretation of provisions N3457/409/38, (National Archives, Kew Garden) http://yourarchives.nationalarchives.gov.uk/index.php?title=Yalta_Conference_in_t he_Crimea_between_the_Soviet_Union%2C_UK_and_US%2C_1945 [accessed October 12, 2011]

Yalta Conference in the Crimea between the Soviet Union, UK and US, 1945, (National Archives, Kew Garden) http://yourarchives.nationalarchives.gov.uk/index.php?title=Yalta_Conference_in_t he_Crimea_between_the_Soviet_Union%2C_UK_and_US%2C_1945 [accessed June 4, 2011]

Program of Czechoslovak government of the National Front of Czechs and Slovaks adopted on April 5th, 1945, in Košice (*Košice Government Program),* *1945, (published informally).* Summary in English is cited in Appendix. http://www.anticomm.co.uk/?p=295 [accessed October 12, 2011]

Potsdam Conference, 1945, (Yale Law School Library) Avalon Project: A decade of American foreign policy 1941-1949. Yale Law School, Lillian Goldman Library, The Avalon Project; Article XII. http://avalon.law.yale.edu/20th_century/decade17.asp [accessed October 12, 2011]

Potsdam Conference, 1945, (Harry Truman Presidential Library) Student Activity: Harry Truman and the Potsdam Conference. The Truman Library http://www.trumanlibrary.org/teacher/potsdam.htm [accessed October 12, 2011]

Potsdam Conference, 1945, (Harry Truman Presidential Library) Truman, H: Handwritten notes of President Truman Notes by Harry S. Truman on the Potsdam Conference, July 16, 1945. President's Secretary's File, Truman Papers. Harry S. Truman Library and Museum. http://www.trumanlibrary.org/whistlestop/study_collections/bomb/large/documen ts/index.php?pagenumber=2&documentid=1&documentdate=1945-07-16&studycollectionid=abomb&groupid= [accessed October 14,, 2011]

Potsdam Conference, 1945, (Department of the Navy) Naval Historical Center. Potsdam Conference, July 16, 1945 to August 2, 1945: Online library of selected images. Events: World War II Diplomacy: http://www.history.navy.mil/photos/events/wwii-dpl/hd-state/potsdam.htm [accessed October 12, 2011]

Nuremberg Trial Proceedings, 1946, (Yale Law School Library) Volume 22: Judgment of the Nuremberg Tribunal from September 30, 1946; Yale Law School; Lillian Goldman law Library; The Avalon Project. http://avalon.law.yale.edu/imt/09-30-46.asp [accessed October 12, 2011]

Agreement of the governments of Czechoslovak Republic and the USSR from November 23, 1945, and Protocol on mining of uranium ore in CSR and supplies to the USSR, 1945. Lepka F: Czech Uranium. Unknown economical and political context 1945-2002

The Washington Treaty, 1949 (NATO web) http://www.nato.int/cps/en/SID-41426331-6494A785/natolive/topics_67656.htm [accessed October 25, 2011]

Government publications, published informally and unpublished

Beneš, Edvard: *Abdication speech from October 5, 1938* (published informally) http://www.fronta.cz/dokument/edvard-benes-posledni-rozhlasovy-projev-5-rijna-1938 [accessed October 12, 2011]

CPSU CC Politburo *Message to Alexander Dubček*, August 13, 1968. http://library.thinkquest.org/C001155/documents/doc46.htm [accessed October 17, 2011]

Darby's Rangers: *WWII's 20.000 MIA. Our missing POWs of WWII* (published informally) http://darbysrangers.tripod.com/id67.htm [accessed October 13, 2011]

Hanson S, Davis M, Altevogt B, Rapporteur; Forum on Neuroscience and Nervous System Disorders: *CNS Clinical Trials: Suicidality and Data Collection: Workshop Summary.* National Academies Press, page 22, Figure 2-1; 2010. http://www.nap.edu/catalog/12829.html [accessed October 13, 2011]

Politbureau: *On the Re-Examination of the Criminal Case against Petr Křivka and Co. December 1957* (published informally) http://www.anticomm.co.uk/?p=241 [accessed October 14, 2011]

The President of Verification Commission Antoni Macierewicz: *Macierewicz Report on liquidation of the Polish Military Information Services ridden with KGB agents* (published informally) http://www.archive.org/details/MacierewiczReportOnLiquidationOfThePolishMilitaryInformationServices [accessed October 14, 2011]

Czech Senate: Committee for petitions: *Senate hearing on the Institute for study of totalitarian regimes, April 2011* (published informally) http://www.anticomm.co.uk/?p=353 [accessed October 14, 2011]

Cabinet Papers: CAB 129/25 Ernest Bevin: *The threat to Western Civilisation.* Cabinet papers, March 1948. (National Archives, Kew Garden) http://www.nationalarchives.gov.uk/documentsonline/details-result.asp?queryType=1&resultcount=1&Edoc_Id=7970998 [accessed October 14, 2011]

Cabinet papers: *Lord Halifax: Anglo-French Conversations (on Czechoslovakia)*, third meeting on **April 29, 1938**; CAB 24/276, (National Archives, Kew Garden) http://www.nationalarchives.gov.uk/documentsonline/details-result.asp?queryType=1&resultcount=1&Edoc_Id=8047496 [accessed October 18, 2011]

Cabinet papers: *Situation in Central Europe*. Memorandum by the Secretary of State for Foreign Affairs. March 22, 1938. CAB 24/276, (National Archives, Kew Garden) http://www.nationalarchives.gov.uk/documentsonline/details-result.asp?queryType=1&resultcount=1&Edoc_Id=8047463 [accessed October 2011]

Committee on Science, Engineering, and Public Policy: *On Being a Scientist: A Guide to Responsible Conduct in Research.* National Academy of Sciences, National Academy of Engineering, and Institute of Medicine, 2009. http://www.nap.edu/catalog/12192.html [accessed October 12, 2011]

HM's Secret Service: *Camp 020,* (National Archives, Kew Garden) http://www.nationalarchives.gov.uk/releases/2007/march/policy.htm [accessed October 13, 2011]

Pool R, Rapporteur; Planning Committee on Field Evaluation of Behavioral and Cognitive Sciences-Based Methods and Tools for Intelligence and Counterintelligence: *Field Evaluation in the Intelligence and Counterintelligence Context: Workshop Summary*; National Research Council, National Academies Press, 2010. http://www.nap.edu/catalog/12854.html [accessed October 13, 2011]

Other published sources

American history: Andrew Jackson: *The petticoat affair - scandal in Jackson's White House.* http://www.historynet.com/andrew-jackson-the-petticoat-affair-scandal-in-jacksons-white-house.htm/2. [accessed October 15, 2011]

Elisabeth Bakke: *The Autonomy discourse in Parliamentary debates during the first Czechoslovak Republic and after the Velvet Revolution.* Department of Political Science, University of Oslo. Published in the scholarly annual Slovakia (Vol XXXVII), numbers 70-71, 2005. (Slovak League of America) http://folk.uio.no/stveb1/Autonomy_discourse.pdf [accessed October 12, 2011]

Banaian, King: *The Demand for Democide: An Instrumental Variables Analysis.* Independent Institute Working Paper Number 43; 2001. http://www.independent.org/pdf/working_papers/43_democide.pdf. [accessed October 14, 2011]

BBC News: *Google releases censorship tools:* http://www.bbc.co.uk/news/technology-11380677 [accessed October 15, 2011]

Bradley CP: *Uncomfortable prescribing decisions: a critical incident study.* British Medical Journal 1992; Volume 304:294-6.

http://www.ncbi.nlm.nih.gov/pmc/articles/PMC1881047/pdf/bmj00058-0034.pdf [accessed October 13, 2011]

Bursík T: *Osud odbojové organizace Černý Lev 777*. Published by OABS MV, Czech Republic, 2007.

Čarnogurský, J: *The Fall of Communism in Czechoslovakia*. http://www.dovekvtisni.cz/download/pdf/static/chapter4.pdf [accessed October 15, 2011]

Catalanová H: *Bolshevik Inquisition (The case of Vladimír Hučín* http://www.jrnyquist.com/bolshevik_inquisition_1.htm [accessed October 17, 2011]

CEFRES Institute Workshop *Film mezi kontrolou a sluzbou moci* (Film between control and servility to power http://www.cefs.cz/dokumenty/cefres.pdf [accessed October 15, 2011]

Clare, JD: *The Yalta Conference: The Big Three during the War:* http://www.johnddare.net/cold_war4.htm [accessed October 13, 2011]

Clifford T: *Law school accused of mafia ties Security threat to state feared amid Plzeň university scandal* http://www.praguepost.com/news/2503-law-school-accused-of-mafia-ties.html [accessed June 3, 2011]

Communist Crimes: *Lithuania. Historical overview 1918-1939*. http://www.communistcrimes.org/en/Database/Lithuania/Historical-Overview [accessed October 13, 2011]

Curtiss, William: *Manufacturing legitimacy: The Czechoslovak Exile Government, 1938-1945*. Williamson College, Williamstown, Massachusetts, April 16 2007. http://library.williams.edu/theses/pdf.php?id=185 [accessed Oct 10 2011]

Czech Republic exits U.S. missile shield plans. Defense News, June 15, 2011. http://www.defensenews.com/story.php?i=6824203 [accessed October 15, 2011]

Czechoslovakia in 1968. That was than 1968; http://thatwasthen1968.com/news/czech1.htm [accessed October 14, 2011, 2011]

Daniliauskas, J: *How significant was Alexander Dubcek in the development of reformist communism?* The University of Hull, Department of politics. The politics of Eastern Europe; 1995. Available at http://works.tarefer.ru/32/100223/index.html [accessed October 14, 2011]

Dickerson, Bryan J : *The liberation of Western Czechoslovakia.* Military History Online. http://www.militaryhistoryonline.com/wwii/articles/liberation1945.aspx [accessed October 11, 2011]

Dolezal, T: Victims of Communism. FCAFA. http://fcafa.wordpress.com/2010/08/15/victims-of-communism-3/ [accessed October 14, 2011]

Druker J: *Czech Republic. Nations in Transit ratings and average scores.* http://www.freedomhouse.org/images/File/nit/2011/NIT-2011-Czech_Republic.pdf [accessed October 15, 2011]

Dudíková A: *Ján Langoš, 59; Slovak dissident opened spy files.* http://www.boston.com/news/globe/obituaries/articles/2006/06/18/jan_langos_59_slovak_dissident_opened_spy_files/ [accessed October 15, 2011]

Ellerman D: *Lessons From East Europe's Voucher Privatization.* http://cog.kent.edu/lib/Ellerman5.htm [accessed October 14, 2011]

Eringer, R: Vaclav Klaus exposed. "The Investigator" Santa Barbara News-Press, December 20, 2008.

http://recolumns.blogspot.com/2010/10/vaclac-klaus-exposed.html [accessed October 14, 2011]

Finch GA: *The Nuremberg Trial and International Law.* Vol 41, No 1 (Jan 1947); 20-37. http://www.st-andrews.ac.uk/itsold/papers/public/miscellaneous/printingproblems/nurem.pdf [accessed October 13, 2011]

Frankel Glen: *Havel details sale of explosives to Libya.* Washington Post, March 23, 1990. http://www.washingtonpost.com/wp-srv/inatl/longterm/panam103/stories/libya0390.htm [accessed October 14, 2011]

Fronta.cz: *Constitutional crisis created by the establishment of Protectorate.* Ústavní vývoj Československý v roce 1938: Part II – Otázka formální kontinuity mezi právním stavem, přivoděným zářijovými a říjnovými událostmi roku 1938 a stavem dřívějším. Available in Czech at Fronta.cz http://www.fronta.cz/dokument/ustavni-vyvoj-ceskoslovensky-v-roce-1938-cast-ii [accessed October 12, 2011]

Havel, V: *Samozvaní samosoudci, jeden z největších úspěchů StB.* Britské Listy. Speech from December 1993. http://blisty.cz/art/32645.html [accessed October 14, 2011]

Hawking S, Mlodinow L: *Stephen Hawking Asks, What Is Reality?* Time Magazine. http://www.time.com/time/arts/article/0,8599,2017262,00.html [accessed October 15, 2011]

Hofhanzl, Č: *Roots of corruption of Czech post-communist democrature.* http://www.konzervativnistrana.cz/nazory/nase-nazory/nazor/article/koreny-korupce-ceske-postkomunisticke-demokratury.html [accessed October 14, 2011]

ILO: *70th Anniversary of the Infamous Munich Agreement.* International Law Observer http://internationallawobserver.eu/2008/09/28/70th-anniversary-of-the-infamous-munich-agreement/ [accessed October 12, 2011]

International Press Institute: *Global network for a free media. Press Freedom audit report – Czech Republic.* IPI Mission, May 2009. http://www.ifex.org/czech_republic/2009/10/15/press_freedom_audit_report_czech_republic.pdf [accessed October 15, 2011]

Jewish Museum in Prague: *History of Anti-Semitism;* presentation in Library Prague 10, June 2, 2011

Kraske M, Puhl J: *Eastern Europe's economic boom: The tiny tigers.* Der Spiegel, December 2005.

http://www.spiegel.de/international/spiegel/0,1518,391649,00.html [accessed October 14, 2011]

Křemen P: *Nikomu jsem neublížil* (I harmed no one). http://www.ceskatelevize.cz/porady/10267494987-nikomu-jsem-neublizil/21056226956/ [accessed October 14, 2011]

Kull S, Ramsay C, Lewis L: *Misperceptions, the Media, and the Iraq War.* The Meaning of American democracy. Political Science Quarterly, Summer 2005.

Lišková M: *Organizace Světlana. Studie o působení protikomunistické odbojové skupiny na Zlínsku v letech 1948 – 1952*, Brno 2011. http://is.muni.cz/th/341711/ff_b/Bakalarska_diplomova_prace.doc [October 14, 2011]

Luba Lesna: *ÚPN: Ján Langoš did not lose Široký file.* The Slovak Spectator. http://spectator.sme.sk/articles/view/26423 [accessed October 18, 2011]

Lukeš I: *A Cold War Dangle Operation with an American Dimension. Operation Kámen. Ensnaring the Unwitting in Czechoslovakia.* Studies in Intelligence – Journal of the American Intelligence Professional. Unclassified articles from Studies in Intelligence Volume 55, Number 1, (March 2011). https://www.cia.gov/library/center-for-the-study-of-intelligence/csi-publications/csi-studies/studies/vol.-55-no.-1/kamen-a-cold-war-dangle-operation-with-an-american-dimension-1948-1952.html [accessed October 14, 2011]

Maštalíř L: *Ján Langoš, former dissident and post-1989 Czechoslovak Interior Minister, dies in an automobile accident.* http://www.radio.cz/en/section/curraffrs/jan-langos-former-dissident-and-post-1989-czechoslovak-interior-ministerdies-in-an-automobile-accident [accessed October 15, 2011]

Mengeles Erben, Documentary of Arte TV, (available on YouTube) http://www.youtube.com/watch?v=dfN3QQnDLjI [accessed October 14, 2011]

Netanjahu B: *Lessons from the Sudetenland.* Koinonia House, http://www.khouse.org/articles/1997/11/ [accessed October 13, 2011]

NNDB profile: *Rachel Jackson.* http://www.nndb.com/people/855/000126477/ [accessed October 15, 2011]

PBS: *WW2 behind closed doors. A problem with Poland.* http://www.pbs.org/behindcloseddoors/episode-1/ep1_problem_with_poland.html [accessed October 13, 2011]

Pekárková, K: *Mass graves in Ďáblice: Čestné pohřebiště popravených a umučených politických vězňů v Praze-Ďáblicích. (Honorary graveyard of political prisoners who were either executed or tortured to death)*. www.arcig.cz/projekty/historseminar/pekarkova.doc [accessed October 14, 2011]

Pospíšil, J: *Světlana prohrála boj, nikoliv válku.* Týdeník Kroměřížska, May 1991. Available at the Museum of Third Resistance, Příbram. Online at http://www.anticomm.co.uk/?p=1097 [accessed October 14, 2011].

Protikomunisticke misto: *Maršál RAF, divizní generál ČSA RNDr. Karel Janoušek.* http://protikomunisticke.misto.cz/svedectvi/5e.htm [accessed October 14, 2011]

Reporters Without Borders: *Journalist Sabina Slonkova convicted for protecting her sources,* 11 February 2009, http://www.unhcr.org/refworld/docid/4993e269c.html [accessed October 15, 2011]

Rosenberg, T: *Overcoming the legacies of dictatorship.* http://www.foreignaffairs.com/articles/50981/tina-rosenberg/overcoming-the-legacies-of-dictatorship [accessed October 14, 2011]

Rummel: *Freedom, democide, war:* http://www.hawaii.edu/powerkills/ [accessed October 15, 2011]

Salpeter E: *Sudeten Germans continue fight for right of return.* Haaretz, September 3, 2003. Available at Haaretz: http://www.haaretz.com/print-edition/features/sudeten-germans-continue-fight-for-right-of-return-1.98974 [accessed October 13, 2011]

Schovánek Radek: *Organizační vývoj technických složek MV 1948-1989* in Securitas Imperii 1 a 2, ÚDV 1994

Serendipity: *Censorship.* http://www.serendipity.li/cda.html [accessed October 15, 2011]

Simon TF: *Milan Rastislav Štefánik.* http://www.tfsimon.com/stefanik-note.htm [accessed October 13, 2011]

Skousen Joel: *Cancelled US missile shield signals new race to war.* World Affairs brief, Rense.com. September 25, 2009. http://www.rense.com/general87/cancel.htm [accessed October 14, 2011]

Spurný J: *Policie jako mocenský nástroj* (Police as a tool of power). Respekt XXII; 16-17, 2011.

Stehlík E: *Příspěvek k historii Czechoslovak Intelligence Organization - CIO (1948-1957).* Museum of Third Resistance. http://www.anticomm.co.uk/wp-content/uploads/2011/05/TAB3h1.jpg [accessed October 14, 2011]

Temné svědectví na Ďáblickém hřbitově. Městská část Ďáblice. http://www.dablice.cz/?view=39,464,0,0,0,0,39,-1&cat=7 [accessed October 14, 2011]

The British Constitution: There is no single document codified as Constitution. History Learning Site. http://www.historylearningsite.co.uk/british_constitution.htm [accessed October 12, 2011]

The Cibulka's list. List of StB confidents obtained by Petr Cibulka and David Eleder; http://www.cibulka.com [accessed October 14, 2011]

University of Liverpool: *Centre for Critical & Major Incident Psychology.* http://www.liv.ac.uk/psychology/ccir/ [accessed October 13, 2011]

University of Liverpool: *MSc 1-year Course Investigative & Forensic Psychology.* http://www.liv.ac.uk/psychology/pg/invforpsy.html [accessed October 13, 2011]

Valdova V, Zverina P: *Case of Jiri Wolf - Personification of Innocence.* http://www.anticomm.co.uk/?p=558 [accessed June 4, 2011]

Valdova, V: *Rogue Czech SF soldiers go to jail.* http://www.anticomm.co.uk/?p=2522 [accessed October 15, 2011]

Vanek J: *Venovano desatemu vyroci tragicke smrti Davida Eledera* (Dedicated to the 10th anniversary of death of David Eleder. http://www.virtually.cz/starydesign/2202/vanek.html [accessed October 14, 2011]

Walton C: *Torture and intelligence gathering in Western democracies.* http://www.historyandpolicy.org/papers/policy-paper-78.html [accessed October 13, 2011]

Ynet News: *Russia to supply Syria with P800 missiles* http://www.ynetnews.com/articles/0,7340,L-3955585,00.html [accessed October 15, 2011]

ABOUT THE AUTHOR

Veronika Valdova was born in Zlin, Czech Republic, and grew up in Wallachia region and adjacent forests. After graduation from the University of veterinary and pharmaceutical sciences in Brno she worked first in animal nutrition and then in pharmacovigilance (drug safety). In November 2006, she left the Czech Republic first for Spain and then for England where she worked in pharmaceutical industry in pharmacovigilance (drug safety). The author is also an outdoor enthusiast and a keen hiker.